SEISMIC SHIFT

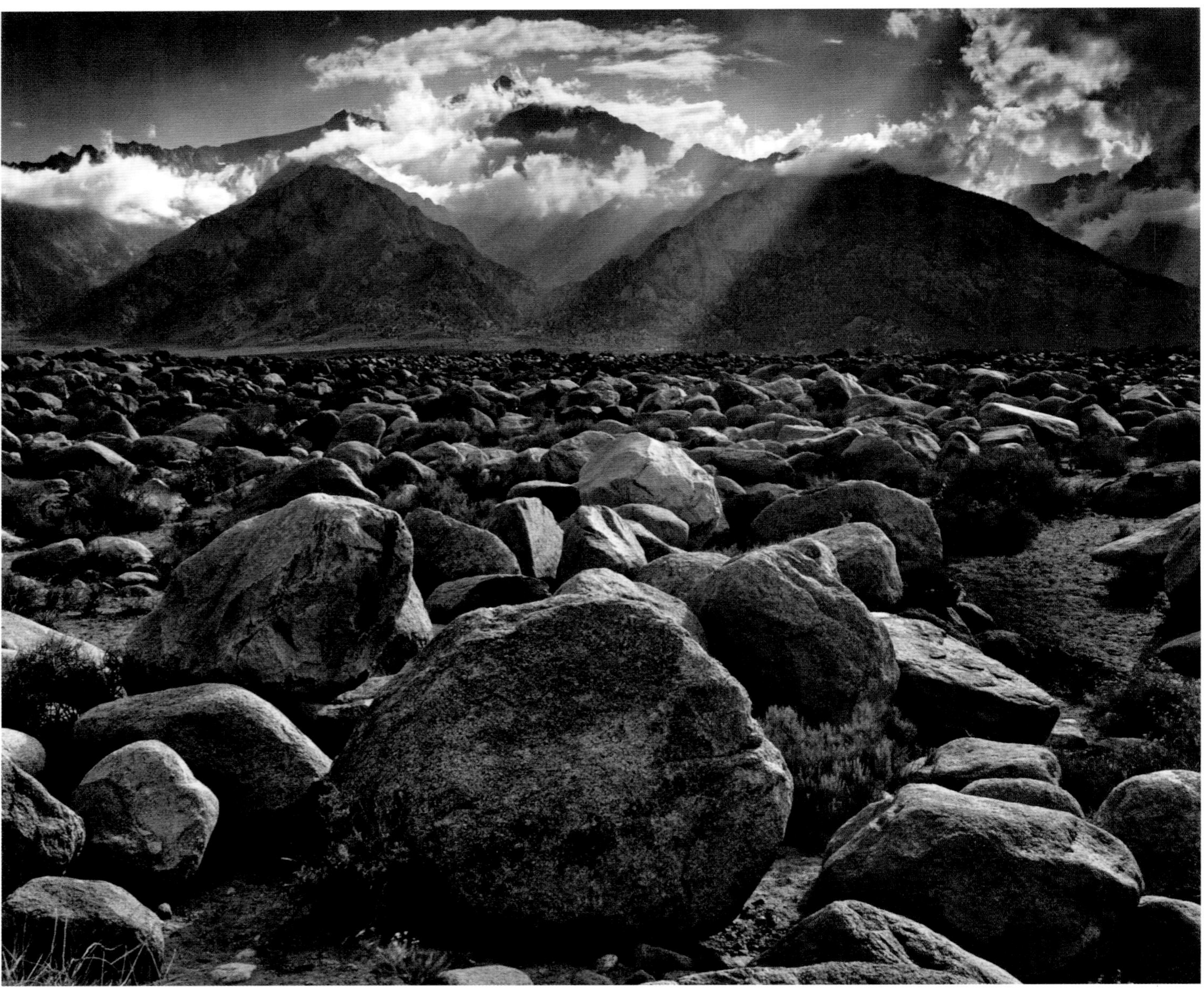

All prints are gelatin silver unless otherwise noted.

^ Plate 1 **Ansel Adams**, Mount Williamson, Sierra Nevada, from Manzanar, California, 1944 (printed 1978), UCR/California Museum of Photography

> Plate 2 **Edmund Teske**, Mono Lake, 1977, composite solarized gelatin silver print, Oakland Museum of California

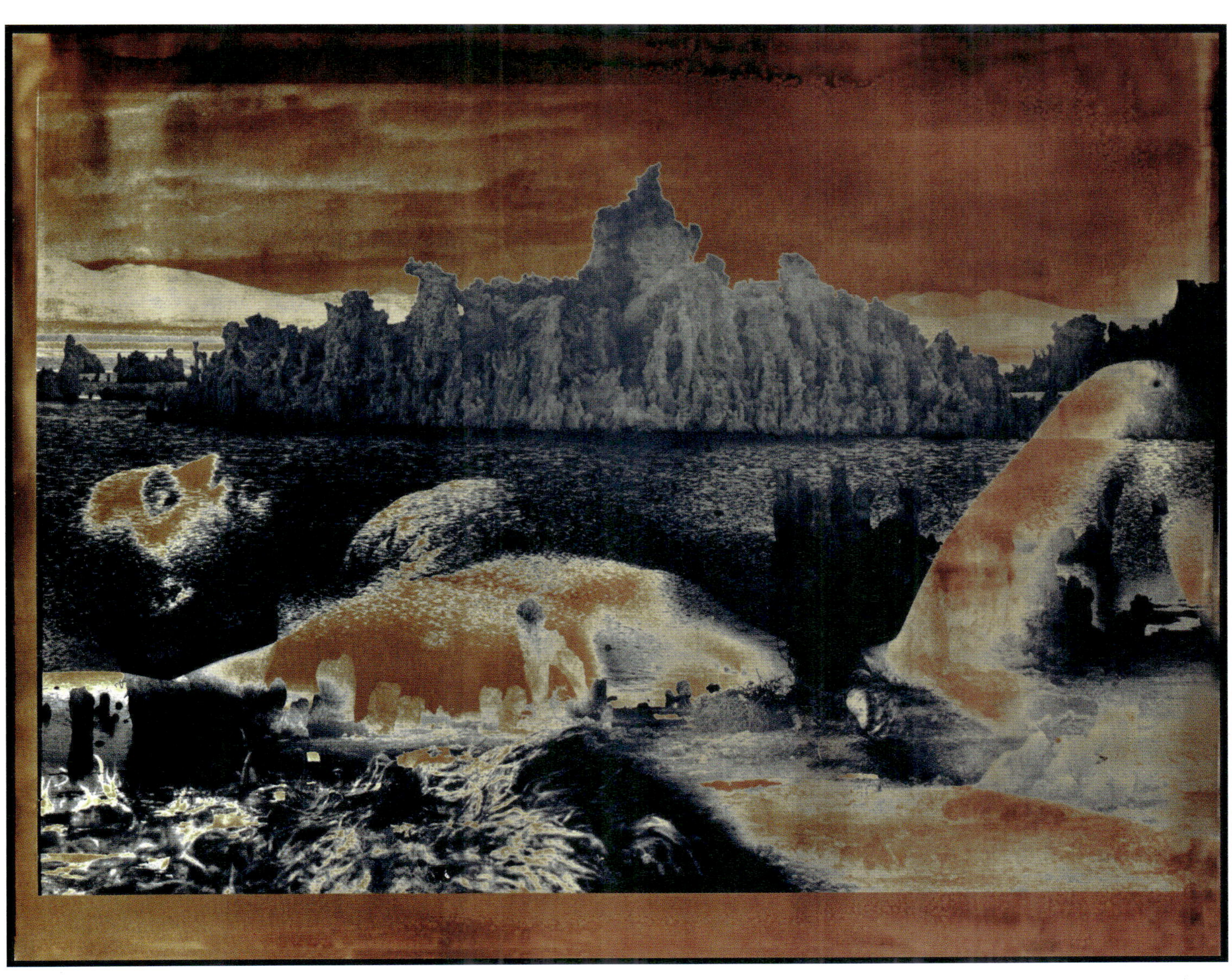

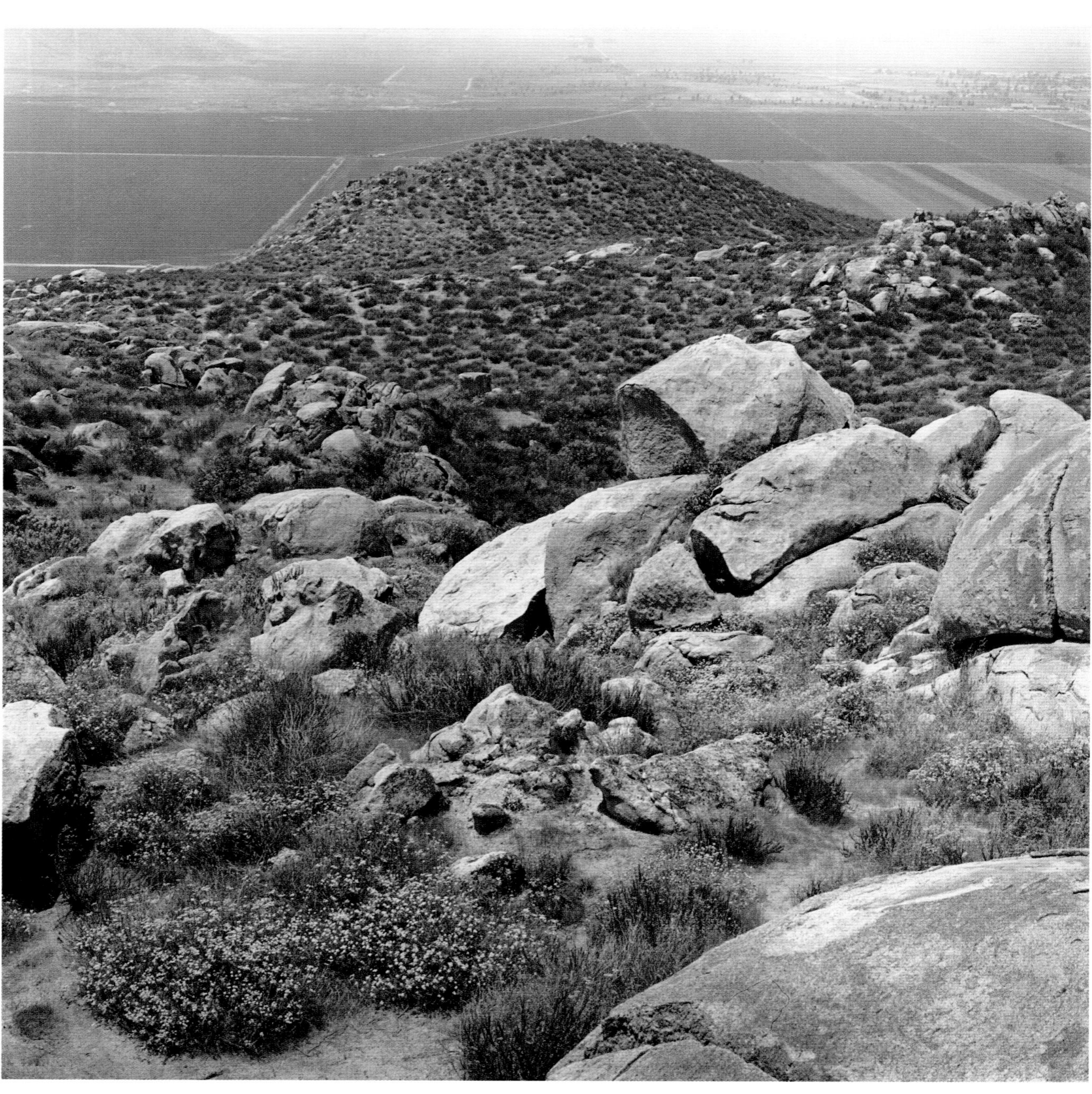

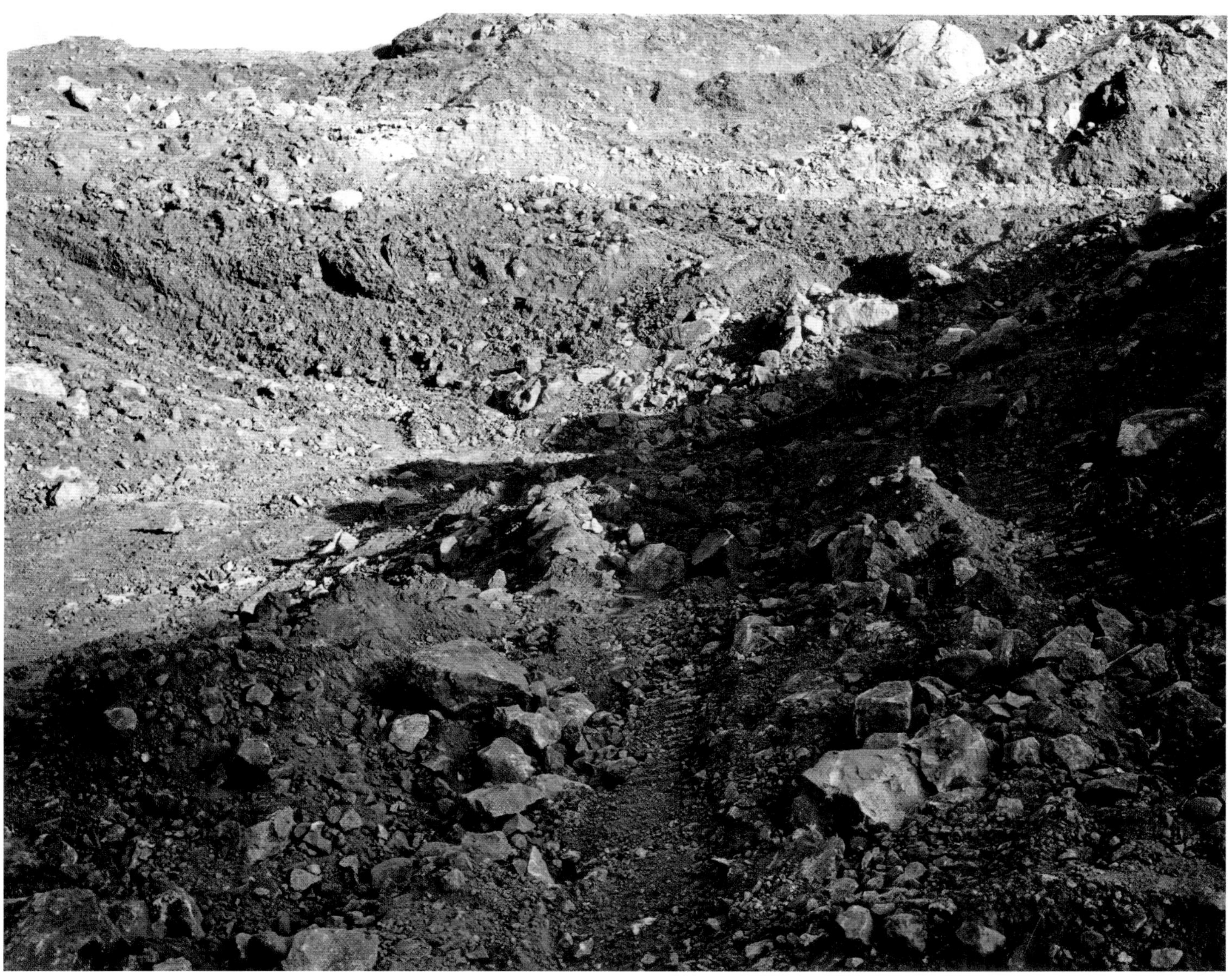

< Plate 3 **Joe Deal**, Hemet, California, 1979, *The Fault Zone* portfolio, UCR/California Museum of Photography

^ Plate 4 **Lewis Baltz**, untitled, Marin County, 1983, *Sideviews* portfolio, UCR/California Museum of Photography

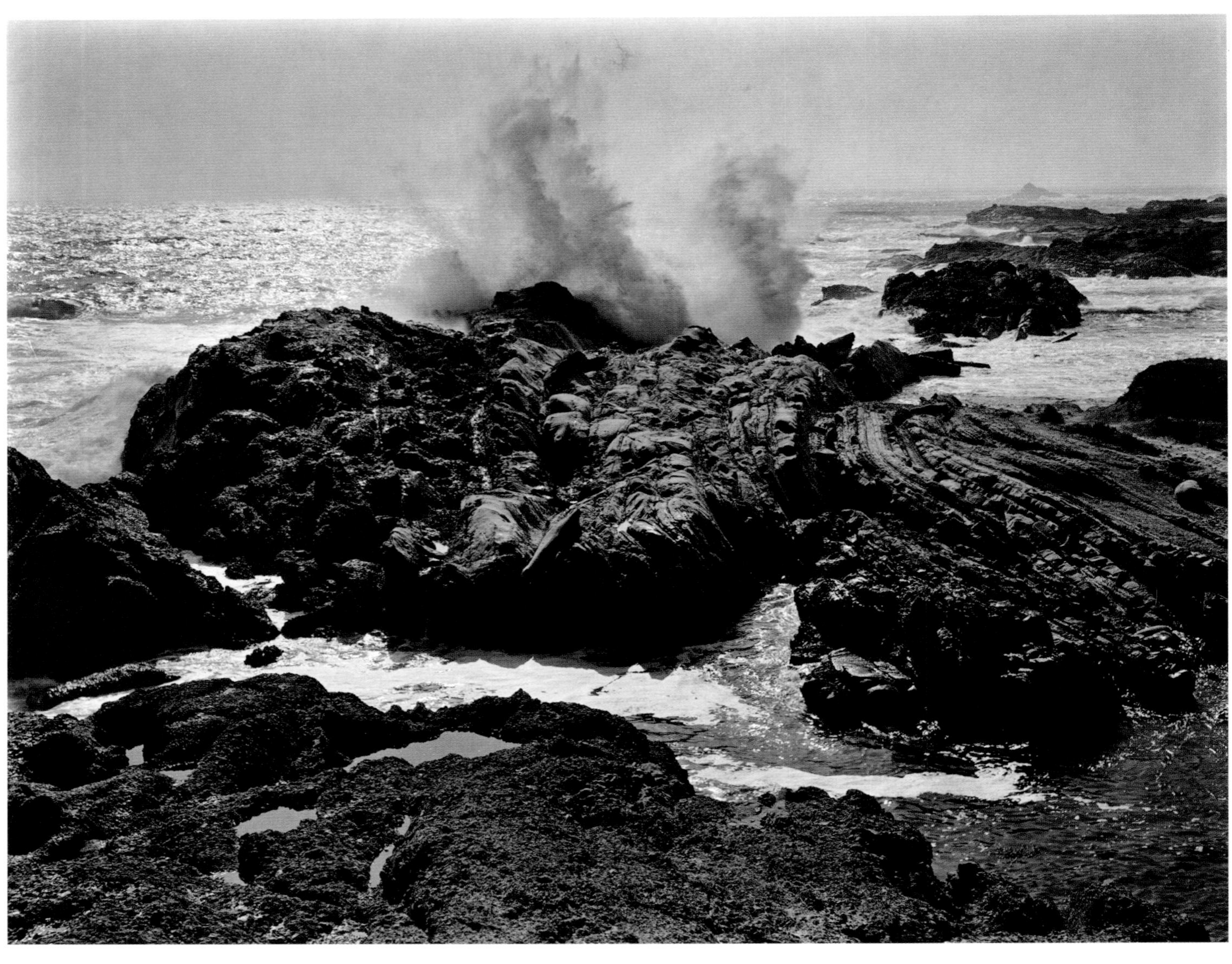

^ Plate 5 **Edward Weston**, Surf, Point Lobos, 1947, UCR/California Museum of Photography

> Plate 6 **Ansel Adams**, Clouds above Golden Canyon, Death Valley, California, 1946, Norton Simon Museum

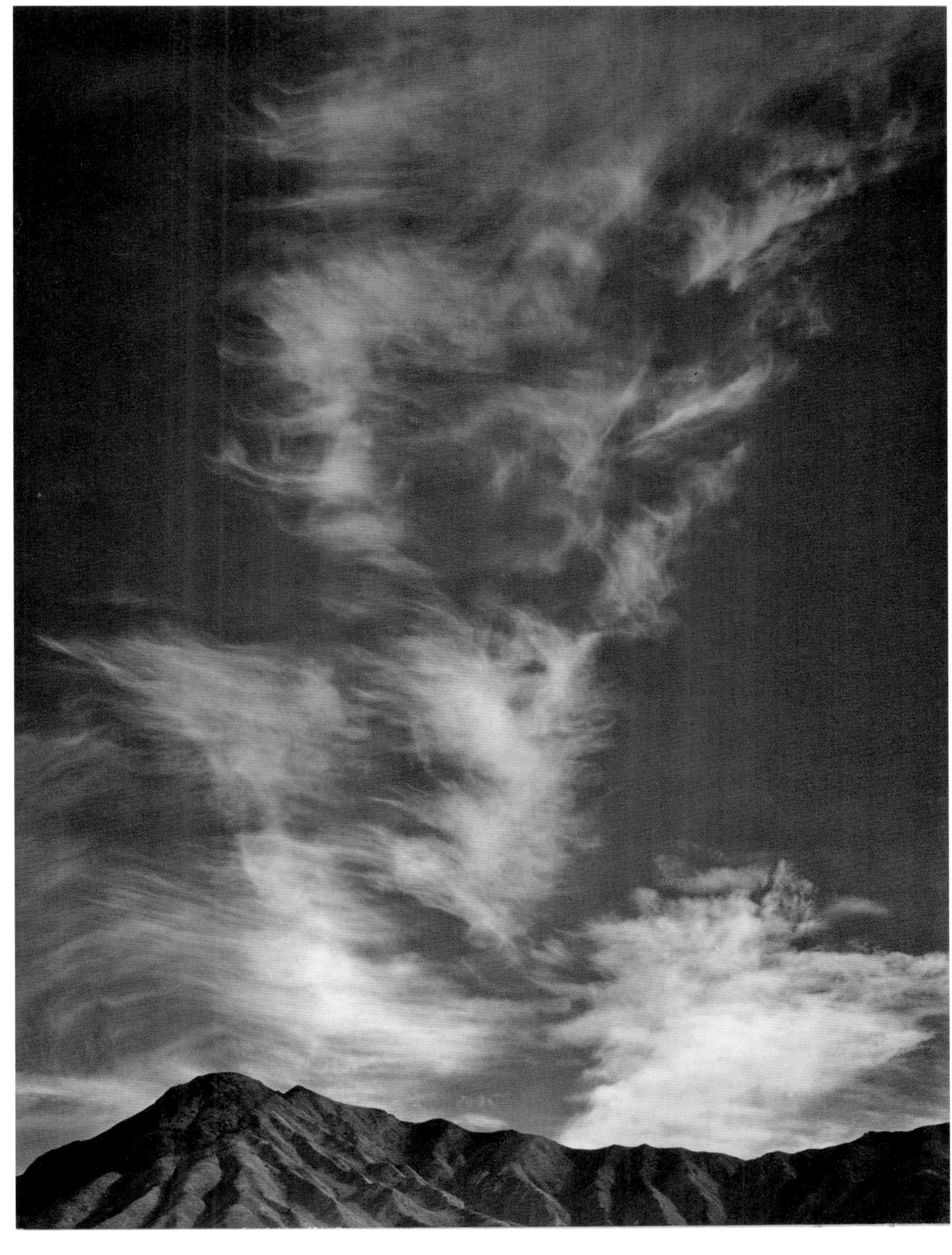

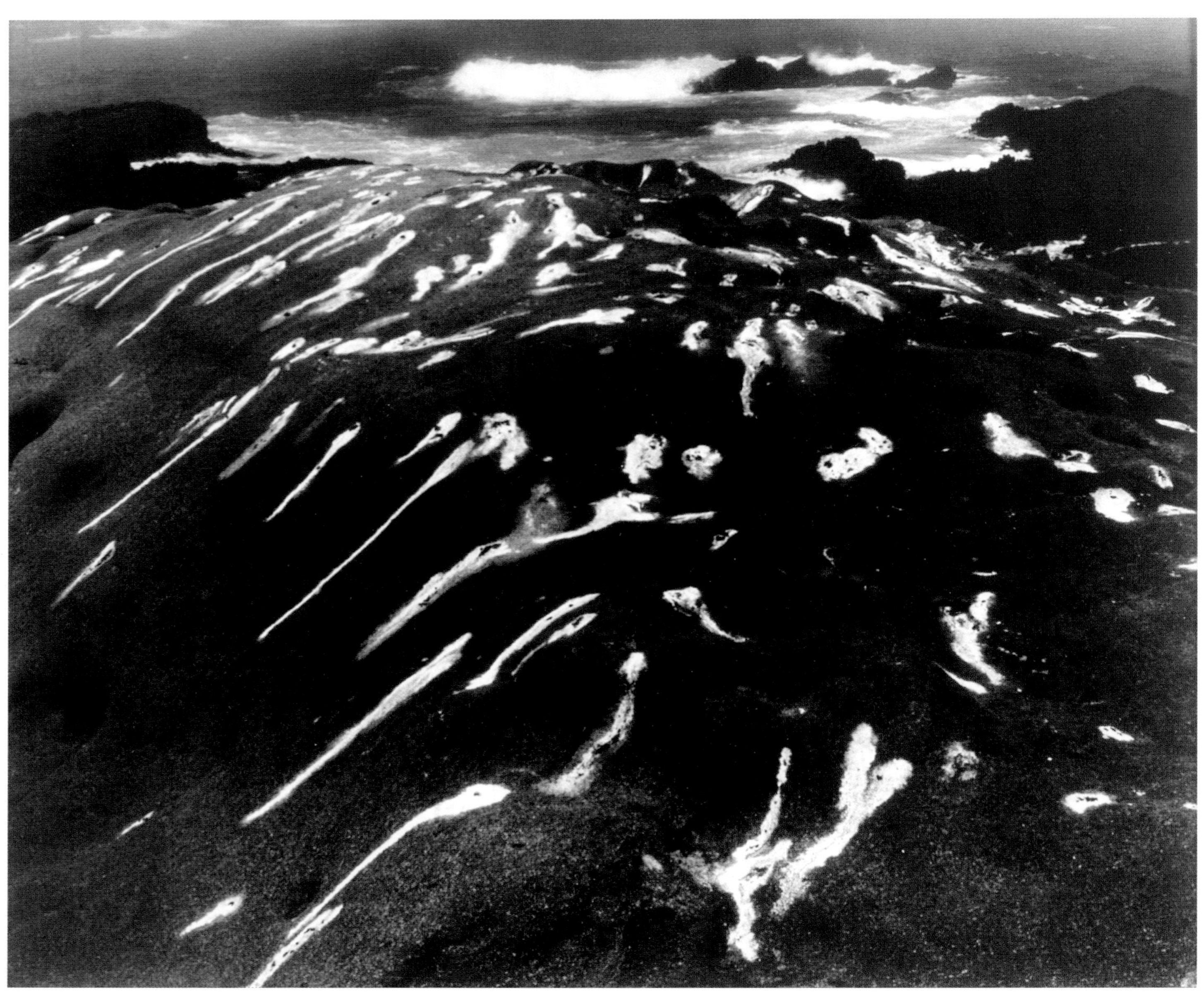

^ Plate 7 **Minor White**, Point Lobos State Park, California, 1951 (printed 1975), Los Angeles County Museum of Art

> Plate 8 **Edward Weston**, North Dome, Point Lobos, 1946, UCR/California Museum of Photography

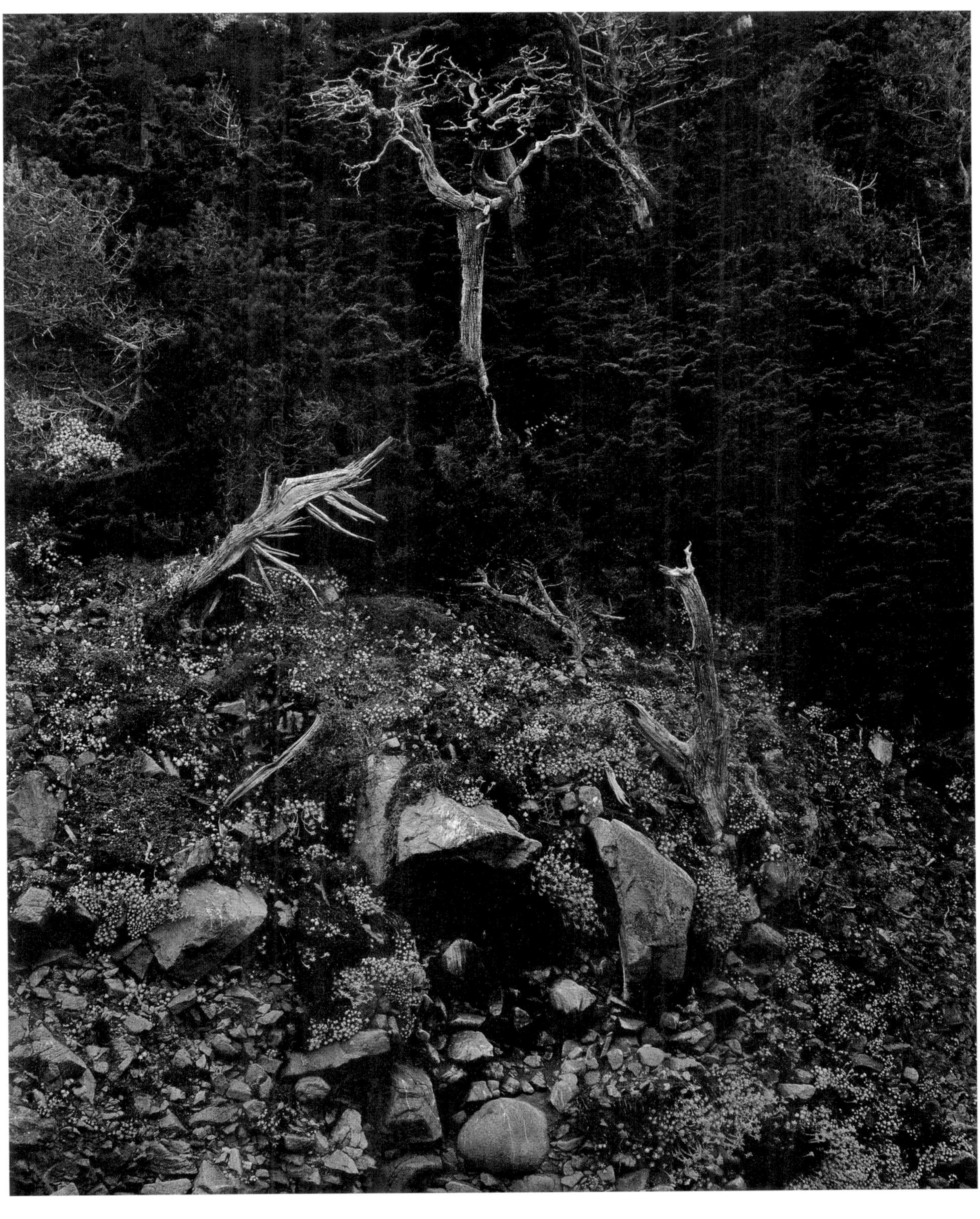

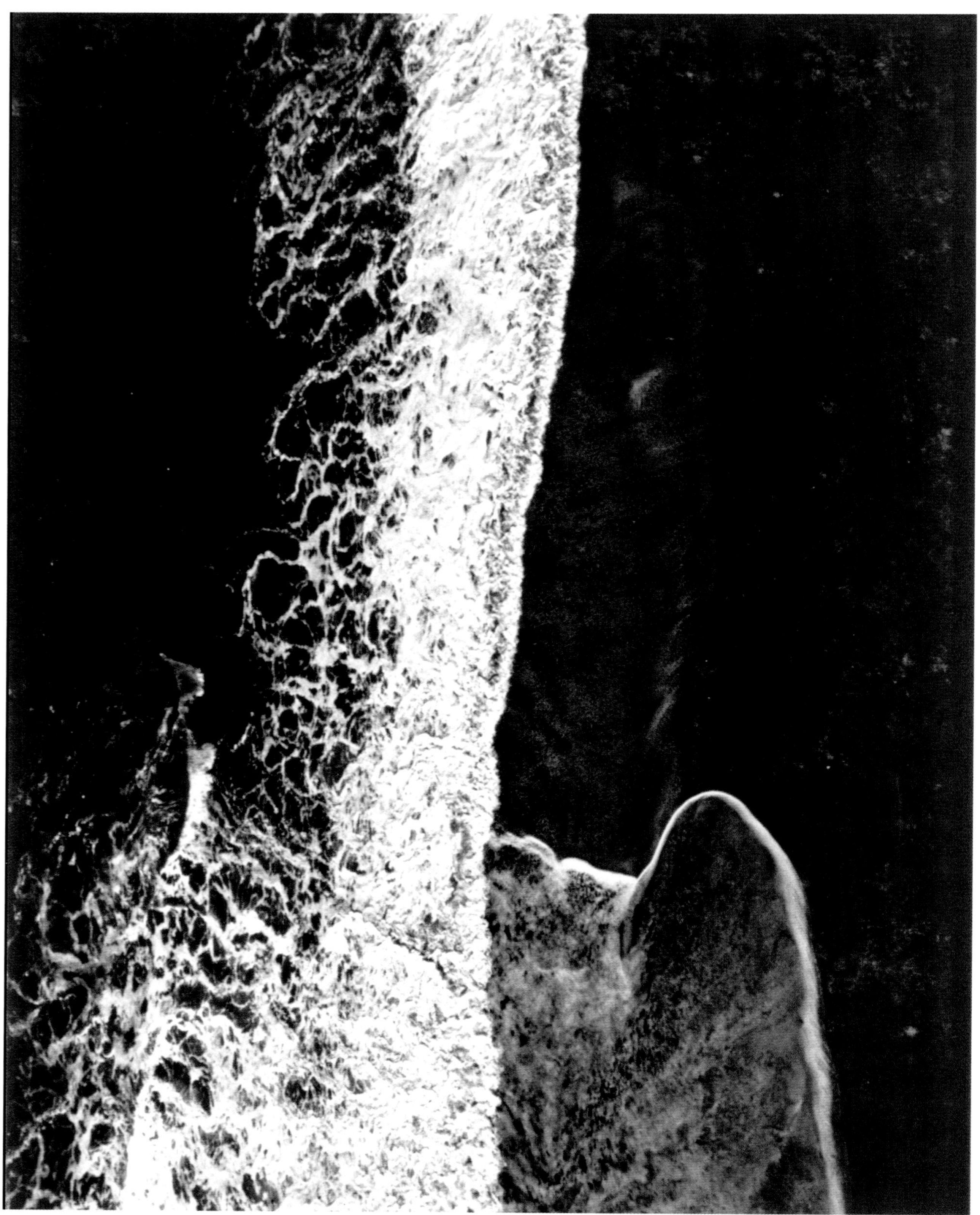

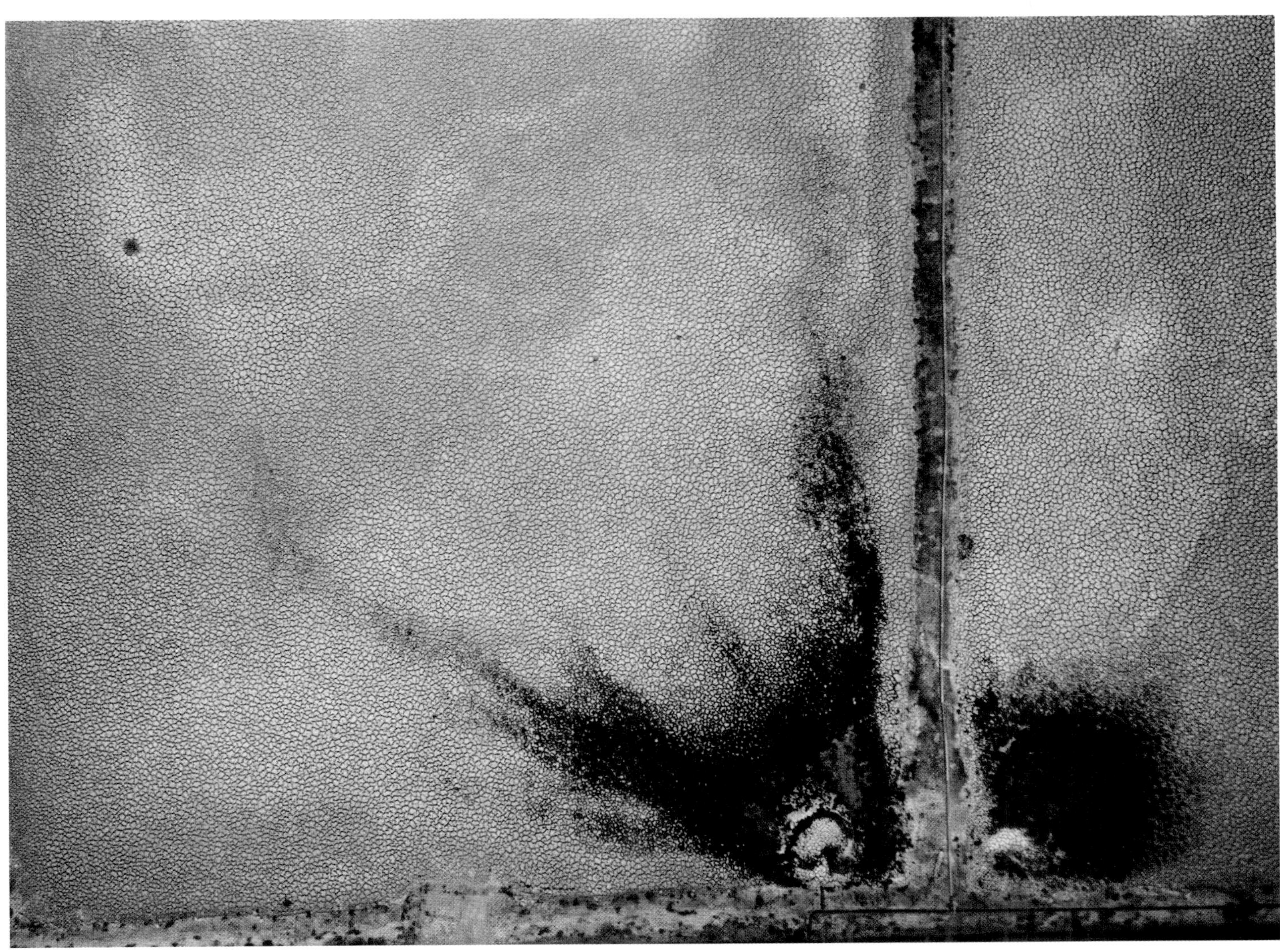

< Plate 9 **Minor White**, San Mateo County, California, in hand-made book *Song Without Words*, 1947, Los Angeles County Museum of Art

^ Plate 10 **William A. Garnett**, Sewage Tank, Santa Paula, California, 1953, J. Paul Getty Museum

SEISM

Lewis Baltz, Joe Deal an

UNIVERSITY OF CALIFORNIA RIVERSIDE **CALIFORNIA MUSEUM OF PHOTOGRAPHY**
PUBLISHED WITH THE ASSISTANCE OF **THE GETTY FOUNDATION**

alifornia Landscape Photography, 1944–1984

SHIFT

Colin Westerbeck with essays by Susan Laxton and Jason Weems

Published in conjunction with an exhibition held at UCR/California Museum of Photography, University of California, Riverside, October 1–December 31, 2011.

Organized and edited by Colin Westerbeck
Designed and produced by Glue + Paper Workshop LLC, www.glueandpaper.com
Printed in China by Asia Pacific Offset
Distributed by RAM Publications & Distribution

ISBN 978-0-9823046-3-1

Both the catalogue and the exhibition *Seismic Shift: Lewis Baltz, Joe Deal and California Landscape Photography, 1944–1984* are part of Pacific Standard Time, an unprecedented collaboration of more than sixty cultural institutions across Southern California, coming together to tell the story of the birth of the LA art scene. Initiated through grants from the Getty Foundation, Pacific Standard Time will take place for six months beginning October 2011.

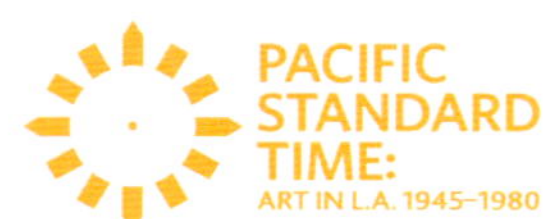

Presenting Sponsors

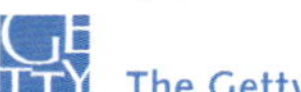

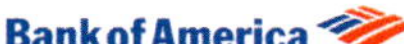

Front cover: (Top) Ansel Adams, Mount Williamson, Sierra Nevada, from Manzanar, California, 1944 (plate 1); (bottom) Joe Deal, Hemet, California, 1979 (plate 3)

Page 17: Photographs of Joe Deal by Herb Quick, 1980

CONTENTS

This exhibition and catalogue are dedicated to the memory of Joe Deal, 1947–2010

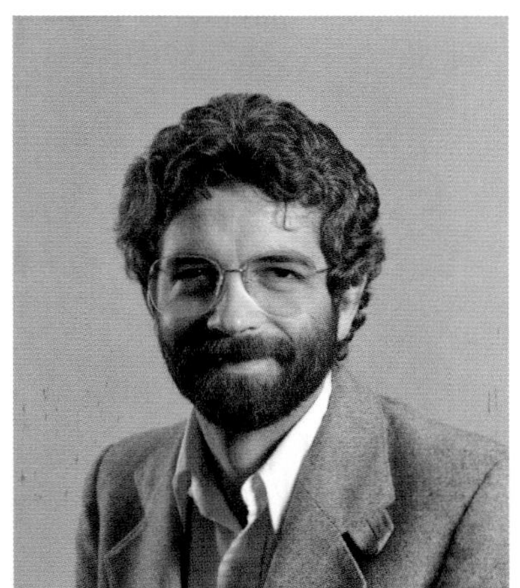

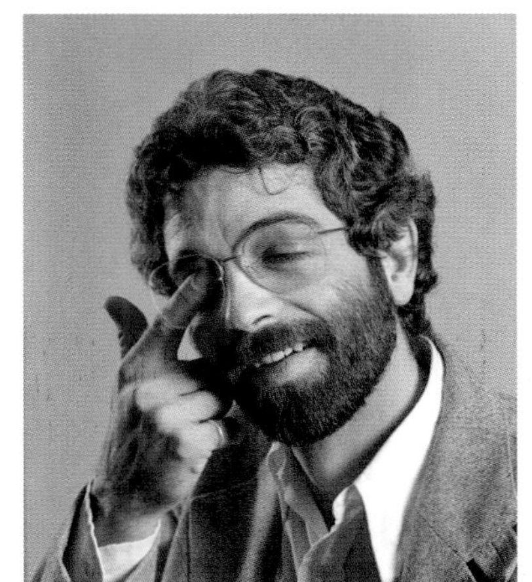

FOREWORD AND ACKNOWLEDGMENTS

As I saw it, the purpose of the Pacific Standard Time initiative was to look at momentous events from a local point of view. This survey of the LA region from the mid-1940s until the early-1980s was intended to reveal not only the repercussions of new developments in the visual arts then, but the origins of such developments. The University of California, Riverside and its California Museum of Photography (UCR/CMP), the latter founded in 1973 as the first free-standing museum in the state devoted exclusively to photography, were at the very least an important crossroads for some seminal photographic careers of the period, including those of Lewis Baltz and the late Joe Deal. Both men played a key role in the formation of the movement that came to be known as the New Topographics, and each did so beginning in the 1970s when they were on the UC Riverside campus—Baltz for several intermittent stays, first in connection with an exhibition and later as a teacher, and Deal as permanent faculty from 1976 until 1989. The work that they and the dozens of other photographers in this exhibition did in California, beginning with Ansel Adams and Edward Weston, influenced postwar landscape photography everywhere.

An exhibition that contains an historical narrative of this complexity (there are 142 photographs by 43 photographers in the checklist) could not have been put together without the help and careful attention of many people. Everyone we approached for advice, assistance or some other form of support responded with enthusiasm and generosity. In early 2010, Getty Research Institute Deputy Director Andrew Perchuk was kind enough to contact me and encourage an application, assuring me that it was still not too late to be considered. Jonathan Green, the Executive Director of ARTSblock here at UCR, and ARTSblock Administrative Director Emily Papavero agreed that we should apply.

By this point, because we were only eighteen months away from the date at which the exhibition would have to open, the application could not have been pulled together had not ARTSblock's Grants Officer, Moira Adams, given it top priority. She cleared the many bureaucratic hurdles that separated the Getty opportunity from UCR applicability. At the Getty Foundation, likewise, Senior Program Officer Nancy Micklewright steered us through the grant application process. When Micklewright left the Getty, the Foundation's Interim Director, Joan Weinstein, stepped in and without skipping a beat guided our application to a successful conclusion. Also facilitating the application was UCR Contract and Grant Officer Mayela Castillo.

As soon as the exhibition grant was completed we applied for the catalogue grant we felt was equally necessary because a written and illustrated narrative, as well as the one on the gallery walls, would be essential to communicating the history of this crucial phase in the development of California landscape photography. Here, especially, Joan Weinstein was understanding of and sympathetic to the need for as generous a grant as was possible. The one other resource needed was a production team with which the catalogue grant would be well and economically spent. I therefore turned to someone with whom I had done a couple of complex catalogues when she and I were both at the Art Institute of Chicago a decade or more ago—Amanda Freymann, now a partner at Glue + Paper Workshop with graphic designer Joan Sommers. Freymann quickly put together a production schedule with Asia Pacific Offset in China.

The remaining personnel necessary to the catalogue were, first, two essay writers in addition to myself, and an editor to sort out the three of us. Because I wanted the catalogue to be an all-UCR publication, I asked Department of Art History Assistant Professors Susan Laxton and Jason Weems to sign on, which both readily agreed to do. Each provided a unique perspective on the exhibition's content, and independent editor Mark Greenberg agreed to whip the drafts created by each of us into shape, which he ably did. Last but not least in the production chain was Theresa Luisotti, whose RAM Publications offered to distribute the catalogue and who aided immensely in obtaining, where Lewis Baltz was concerned, permissions, reproduction files and a key loan.

Once the funding had been secured for both exhibition and catalogue, we worked with Gloria Gerace, the Managing Director of the Pacific Standard Time project at the Getty, whose guidance in coordinating the efforts of the many art institutions involved was always encouraging and positive. She was open to our suggestions, yet always ready to give needed advice. Once the funds were available, ARTSblock Administrative Assistant Cynthia Cardenas handled the endless paper work with efficiency, and Budget Analyst Terrie Boudreaux managed the spending of the funds and keeping of the accounts with her usual professionalism and cheerfulness.

Among the most urgent expenditures was to hire Research Assistants to generate an up-to-date bibliography. Three UCR students served in that capacity: Master's Degree candidates Sarah Bay Williams and Harmony Wolf along with undergraduate Maxine Umali, who proved to be the most persistent and helpful of all. The full-time team I had working with me at UCR/ CMP consisted of Assistant Curator Kristine Thompson and Curator of Collections Leigh Gleason, both of whom dedicated themselves unstintingly to the project in addition to keeping up with all their usual chores. Thompson took on the crucial task of obtaining all rights permissions and reproduction files for both the plates and the essay illustrations in the catalogue, working with Gleason, who is the official Registrar for UCR/ CMP, in setting up the complex schedule of loan requests for the exhibition. Thompson's contribution was the most taxing, and she rose to the challenge with a dedication that made her more than just an assistant on *Seismic Shift*; she was a resourceful collaborator who talked out with me—and often innovated herself—the policies and procedures we needed to put in place as we went along. In truth, Gleason contributed as much to our mutual project despite many other demands on her time.

Exhibition Designer Jeff Cain pitched in early on by taking some vague visions I had for a title wall and exhibition installation and turning them into an elegant design that, submitted as part of our application to the Getty Foundation, helped in securing our grant. Cain also helped to realize the exhibition, not only by both supervising and assisting in building out the gallery space and installing the exhibition, but by working with campus electricians on a long-overdue upgrade to our lighting system. In the installation phase, Cain was ably assisted by Preparator Jacob Leonard, who also did the framing of the prints with his customary care. Director of Digital Media Georg Burwick not only provided the impeccable services he and his crew always do on the museum's website, but also programmed the wall of touch-screen monitors so visitors to the exhibition can page through photographic books of the period.

Finally, enormous appreciation is extended to all of the museums, private collections and photographers who responded to our requests for loans. Chief Curator Carol Tognieri at the Norton Simon Museum was the first to agree to an extensive list of key loans; thanks to her generosity of spirit, our dealings with the Norton Simon Museum provided a model for our efforts elsewhere. Equally responsive with her invaluable advice, access to her Study Room and generous loan policy was was Britt Salvesen, Department Head and Curator of the Wallis Annenberg Department of Photography at the Los Angeles County Museum of Art, whose Curatorial Assistant Eve Schillo also gave freely of her time and assistance. At the J. Paul Getty Museum, Senior Curator Judy Keller and Associate Curator Anne M. Leyden patiently shepherded our loan request through a complex process. During a visit to the Study Room at the Center for Creative Photography, and in the follow-up loan requests, Acting Senior Curator Rebecca Senf and Registrar Trinity Parker responded with gracious help. At the Orange County Museum of Art, Associate Registrar Dianna M. Santillano expedited our request for the loan of a selection of Lewis Baltz's series *New Industrial Parks near Irvine, California*. And at the Oakland Museum of California, Curator of Photography Drew Johnson expedited the loan of a single but essential Edmund Teske print.

Besides Theresa Luisotti at Gallery Luisotti, two other commercial galleries helped us tremendously. One was San Francisco's Fraenkel Gallery, which, through the good offices of Director Frish Brandt, Artist Liaison Peter Colon and Rights and Reproductions contact Carin Johnson, provided both the loans and the reproductions of key Robert Adams work. The other was the Robert Mann Gallery in New York, which administers the estate of Joe Deal. Private collections and collectors were equally generous. The Southern California collections of David Knaus, Sally Stein and Amy Harrison each provided us with loans, as did The Black Dog Collection in San Francisco. Then there were the photographers themselves who offered us their work either as vintage prints or newly minted ones from the original negative. Those who gave generously of their own photography in this way were Laurie Brown, John Divola, Sant Khalsa, Leland Rice, Grant Rusk, Phel Steinmetz and Henry Wessel.

Finally, I want to express my personal gratitude for the time that both Lewis Baltz and Joe Deal gave to providing the interviews excerpted in this catalogue. Art Institute of Chicago Curator of Photography Matt Witkovsky interviewed Baltz, who then edited the selections for this publication. I conducted the interview with Joe Deal only a month before he died. The focus, lucidity and energy he displayed inspired me to move forward with this exhibition.

It seems fitting to end here, with the photographers, as their work was also the beginning of the history that this exhibition narrates. Between the multiple acts of creation from which the history itself was formed and the present exhibition that attempts (however inadequately) to sum it all up, a great many other people were also involved. They are the fellow curators, gallerists, collectors and professionals in allied fields who are also being thanked here for their dedication and their generous support.

Colin Westerbeck, Curator of the Exhibition

Lewis Baltz: When I was 12 years old, I began to photograph seriously... I loved the medium—as a medium. I didn't like the world of photography. I didn't like the culture of photography. I feel the same way today. I don't think it's changed—I don't think the culture has changed as much as it thinks it has, and my feelings toward it haven't changed either....

There was this mythology around Edward Weston. He was an enormously romantic figure. He was sort of a man alone in the world, and against the world. He took off to Mexico. He had beautiful women, at least, he had one beautiful woman I can think of—extraordinarily beautiful. Lived a Walden-like existence on one of the most beautiful pieces of land in the United States and made ... images that were wonderful and underappreciated. I had endless admiration for him, his work and, above all, his romantic myth. On the other hand, there was Robert Frank, gritty, alienated, and way, way outside the mainstream of 1950's American society. But for me, both brought the same existential message: It was a very romantic thing to be an artist. It was a cool, a noble profession, unlike, for example, business.

On November 15 and 17, 2009, Art Institute of Chicago Curator of Photography Matthew S. Witkovsky interviewed Lewis Baltz at Baltz's home in Paris, acting on commission for the Archives of American Art (AAA). These excerpts are drawn from that as yet unpublished interview, which will be available in the future on the AAA website.

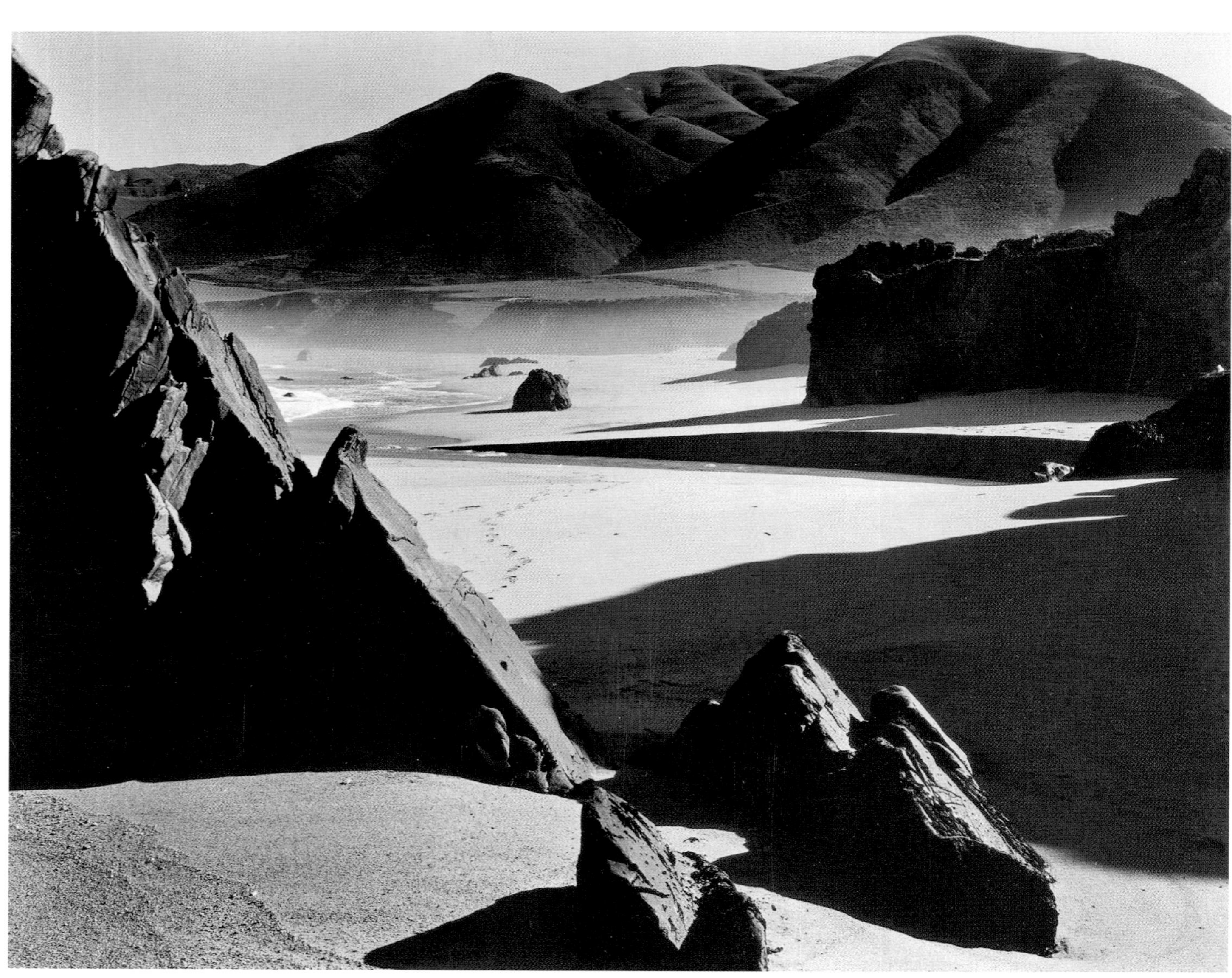

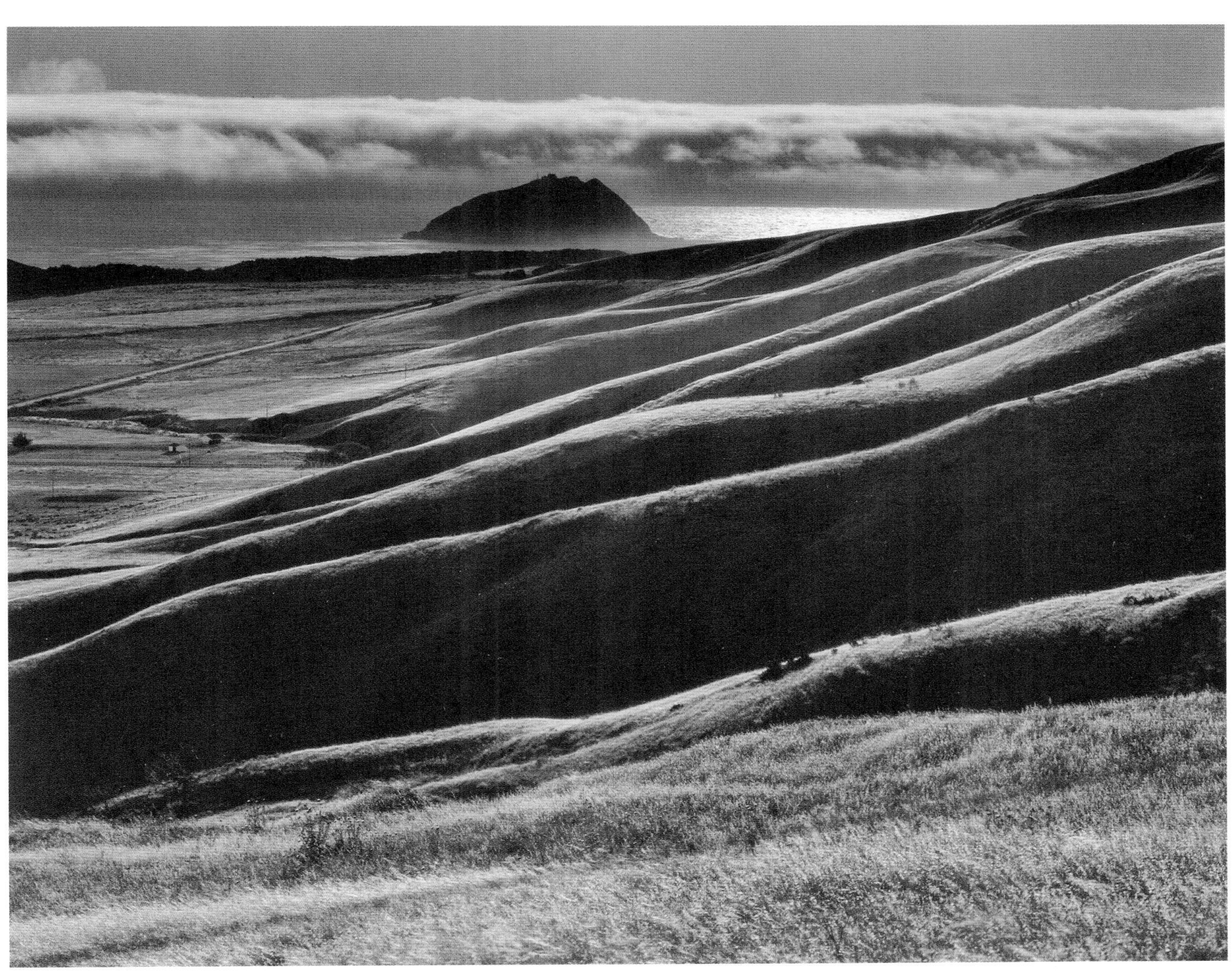

< Plate 11 **Brett Weston**, untitled (Garrapata Beach, California), 1954, Norton Simon Museum

^ Plate 12 **Brett Weston**, untitled (Point Sur and Fog Bank), 1964, Norton Simon Museum

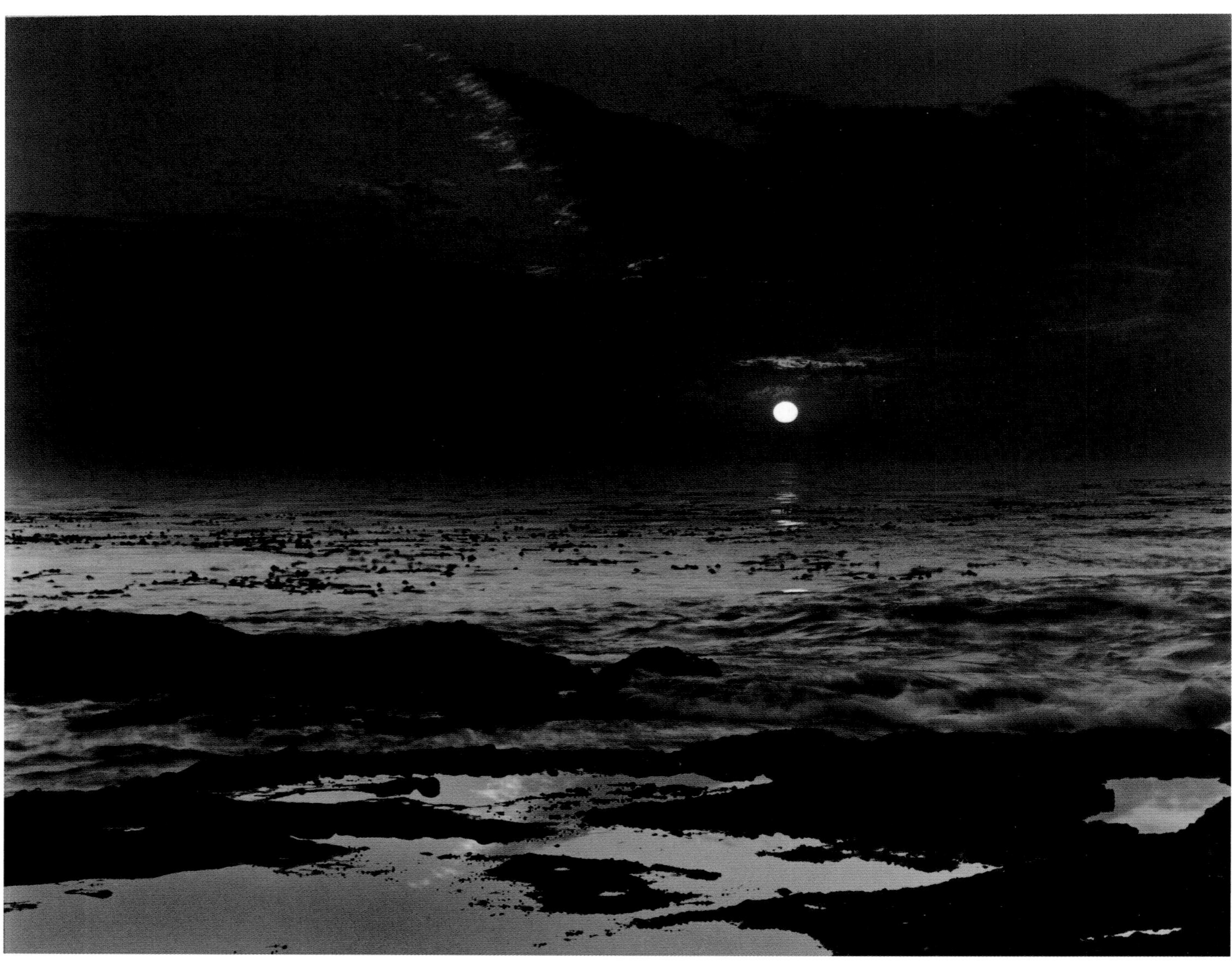

^ Plate 13 **Wynn Bullock**, Sunset, Big Sur Country, 1957, UCR/California Museum of Photography

> Plate 14 **Edmund Teske**, untitled, 1962, composite solarized gelatin silver print, Los Angeles County Museum of Art

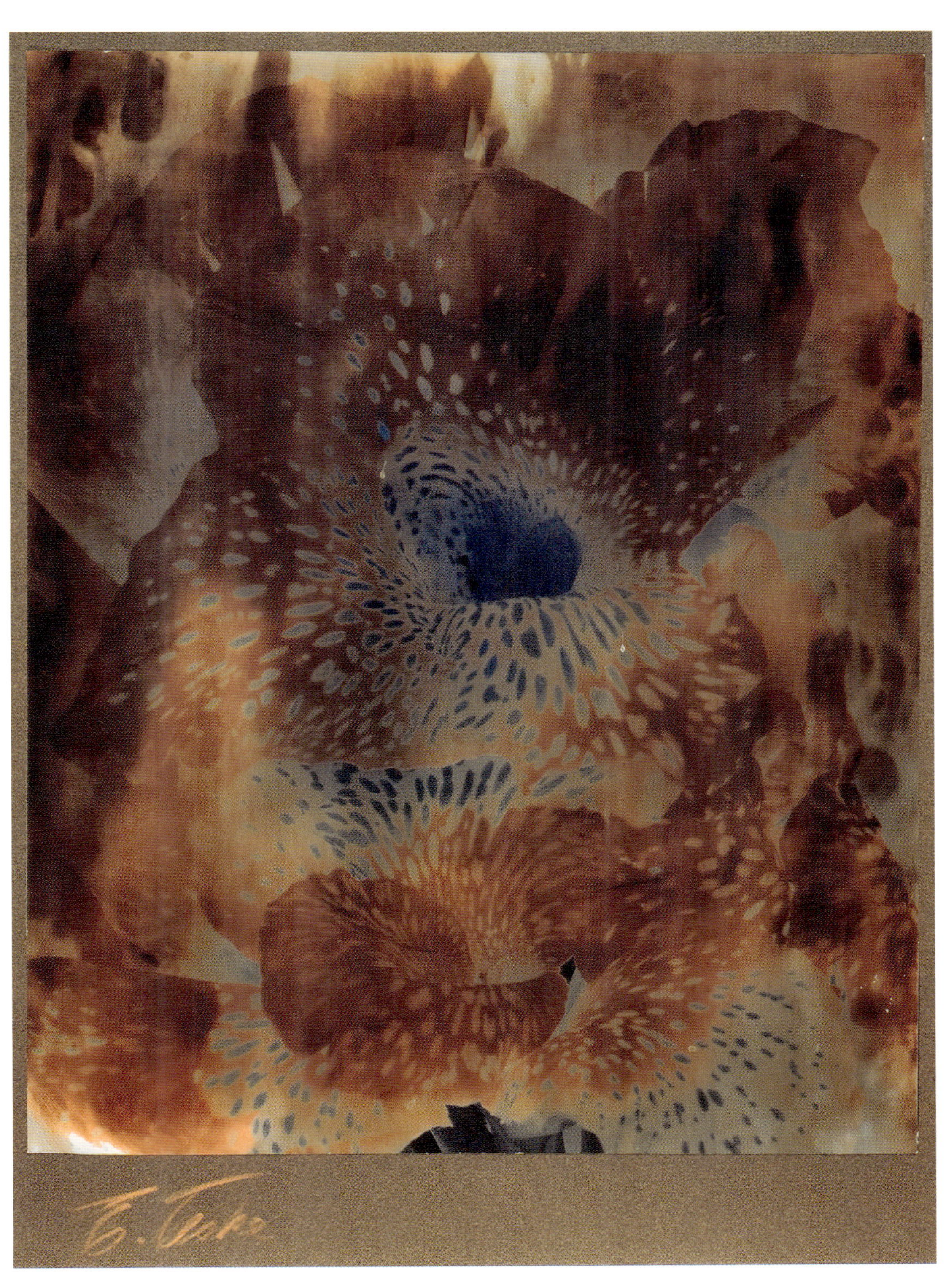

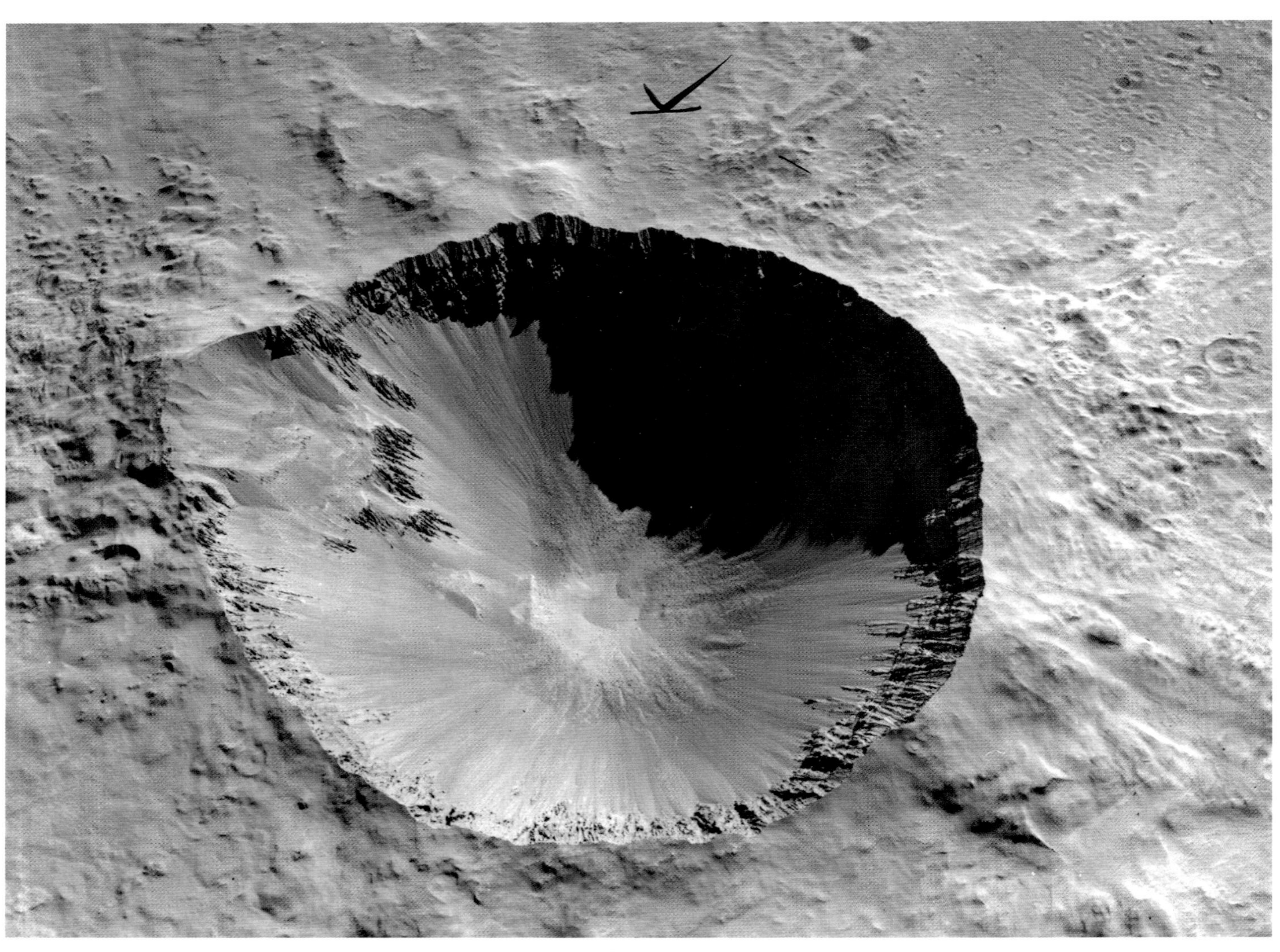

^ Plate 15 **anonymous**, Atomic Crater, 1962, Collection of David Knaus

> Plate 16 **Ruth Bernhard**, Trees Reflected in Shaving Mirror, 1968, Norton Simon Museum

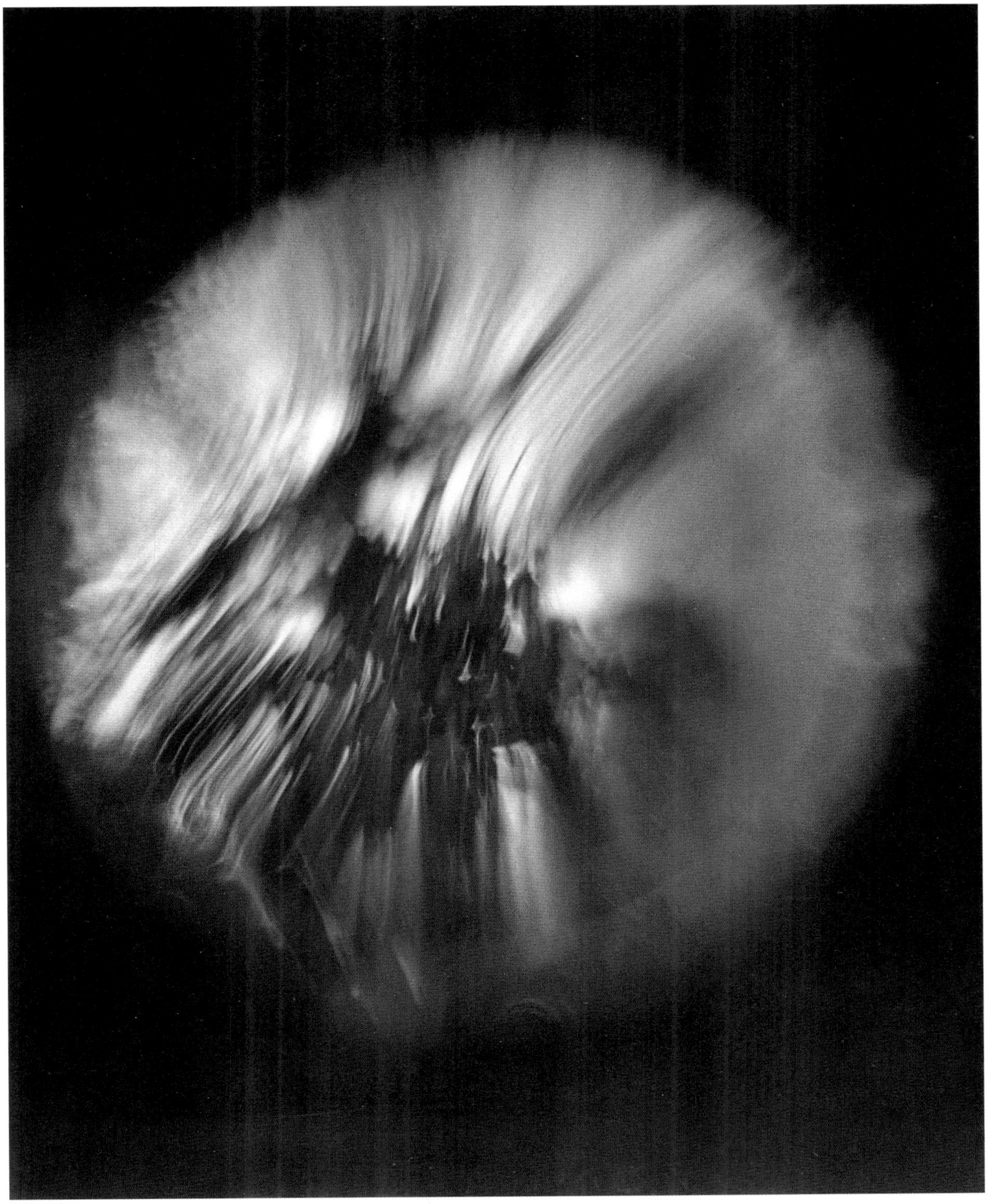

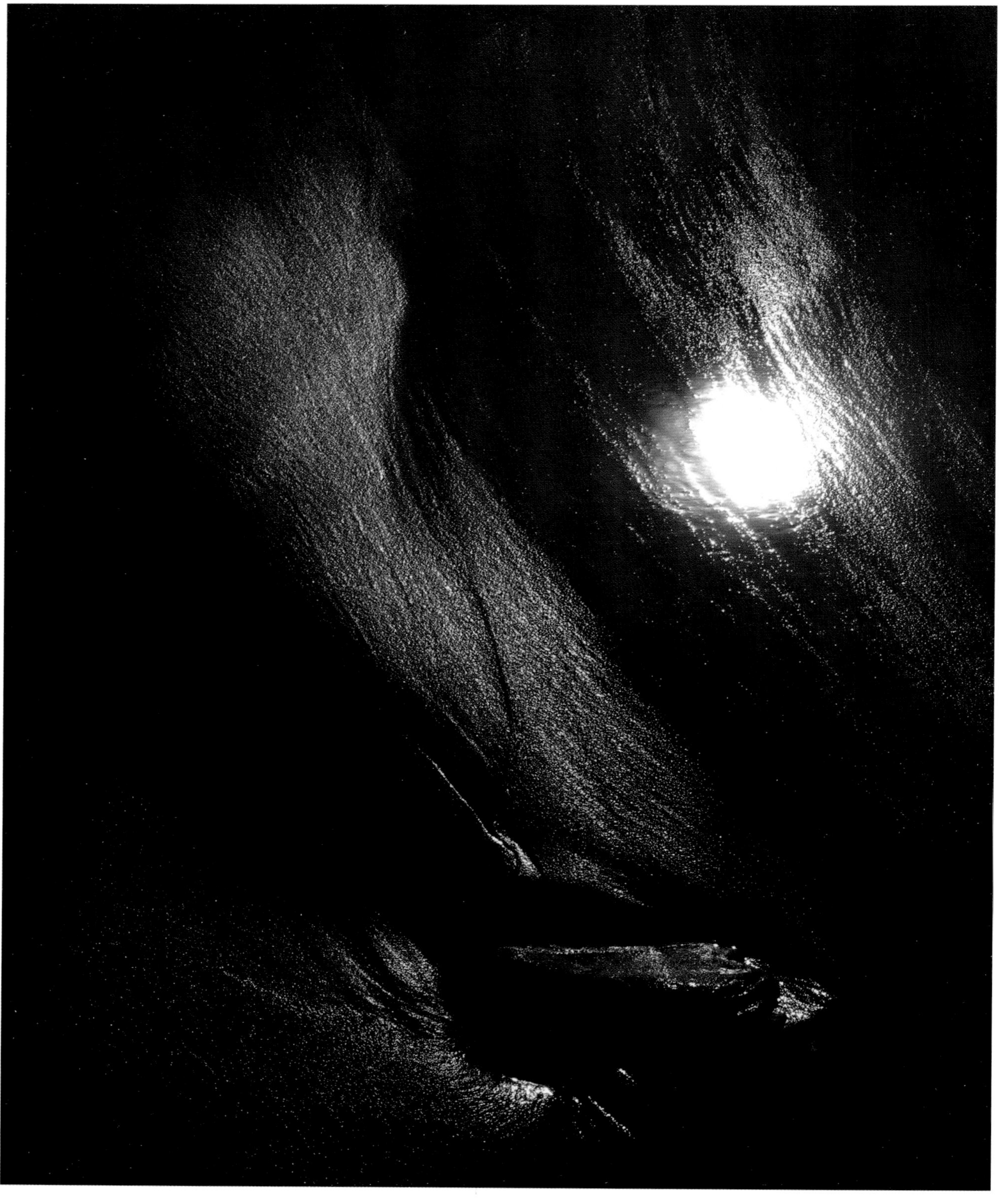

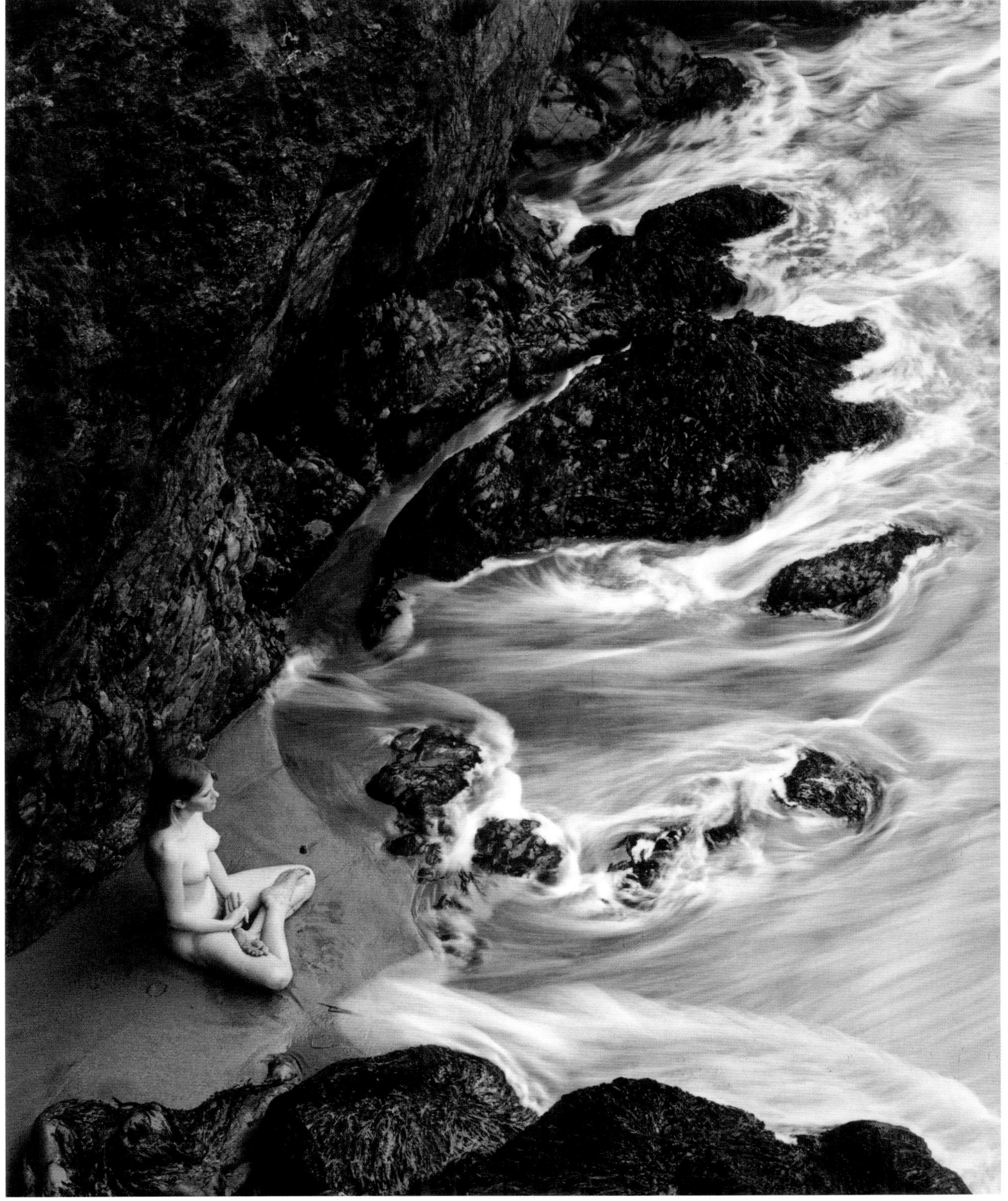

< Plate 17 **Oliver Gagliani**, untitled (Looks Like Sun Shining on Wet Sand), 1964, Norton Simon Museum

^ Plate 18 **Wynn Bullock**, Girl on Beach, 1968, Center for Creative Photography: Wynn Bullock Archive

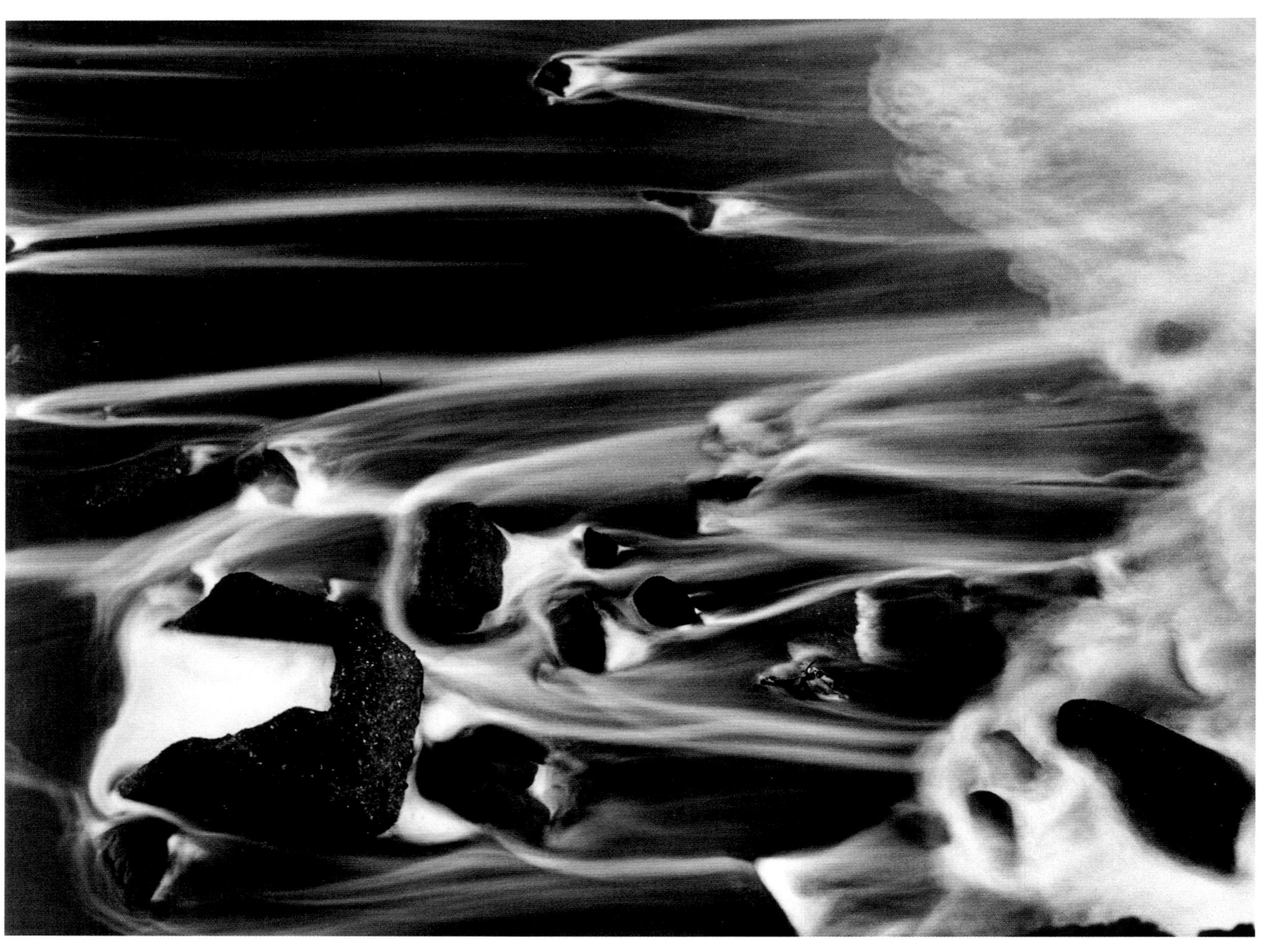

^ Plate 19 **John William Nagel**, untitled (Long Exposure, Mussel Rock, Daly City, California), 1968/70 (printed 1971), Norton Simon Museum

> Plate 20 **Robert W. Fichter**, Desert Smoke with Robot, Walter Chappell and Robbert Flick, 1969, cyanotype, Norton Simon Museum

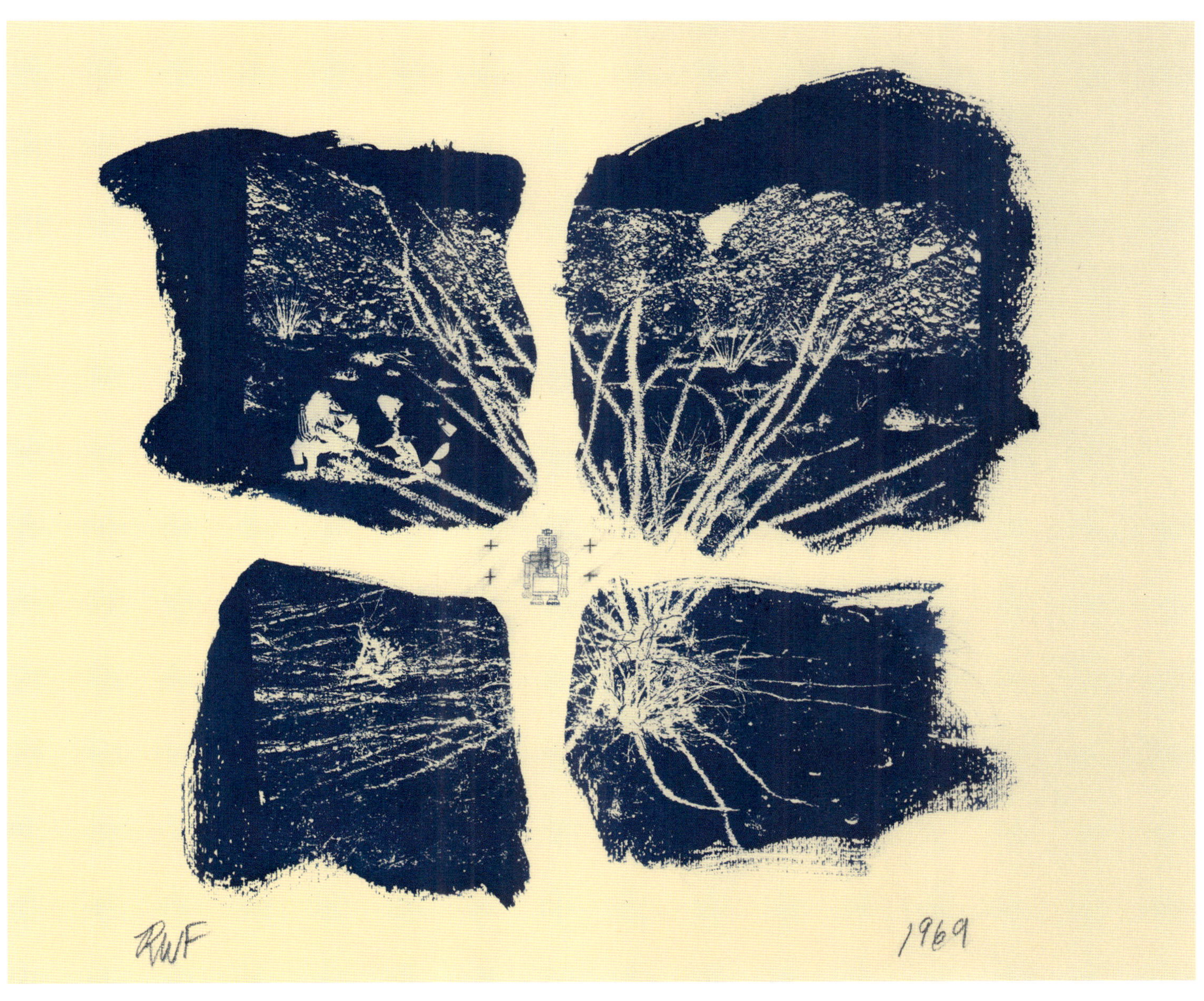
RWF
1969

Joe Deal: The reason I wanted to photograph suburbia was I grew up in the suburbs and I wanted to photograph what I knew. But I didn't want to make fun of it. So one day, in Albuquerque, a professor of mine asked me to work on a poster. The architecture department was sponsoring a competition about how you build in the desert, so he wanted a photograph of building in the desert. I thought, I want to go out and photograph a rock in the desert and then impose a window on it. I just went as far out of town as I could, past the outskirts, to find a rock, basically.

I stood up on a hillside and looked down on Albuquerque, and it just startled me that here, spread before me, was what I'd been looking for in photographing suburbia: that it wasn't just one house, and my interest wasn't in architecture—that I had been going the wrong direction with it, trying to photograph the buildings. I wanted to photograph the landscape, and the buildings became part of the landscape.

That's how that work started. I had no intention of turning my back on California landscape photography traditions or anything of the sort. I was just making work, and that's what it turned out to be.

From an oral-history interview with Joe Deal, May 13 and 14, 2010, conducted by UCR/ California Museum of Photography Director Colin Westerbeck at Deal's home in Providence, Rhode Island. The full interview will be donated to the Archives of American Art and made available on its website.

COLIN WESTERBECK

Epicenters: How the California Landscape Slid South

Introduction

In 1979, Ansel Adams received a letter from a photographer a generation younger than he that began with an apology. The writer hoped his "note" wouldn't be just another "fan letter." In the face of the current deterioration of the Western landscape, the writer said, Adams's photographs "have rescued me often from my own despair" (fig. 1, pls. 1 and 6). He was grateful for Adams's vision of "a cleaner world" and the reassurance that such a world "is eternal, no matter what happens to be out in front of us at the moment." The writer concluded by apologizing again, this time for being an "upstart, albeit obscure, running around with the same name, doing landscapes," and he signed the letter "Bob Adams."

Replying to Robert Adams's letter, Ansel reaffirmed the "positivistic attitude in my own work."[1] One California prospect about which Ansel was not enthusiastic, though, was Los Angeles, where he had taught at the Art Center School from 1940 until 1942.[2] Robert has to have been aware of Ansel's dislike of Los Angeles because his letter mentions his "well thumbed" copy of Ansel's 1960 book with Nancy Newhall, *This is the American Earth*, in which Ansel refers to Los Angeles as the "Hell we are building here on earth."[3] It's an attitude Robert shared, for when he wrote to Ansel he was working on an LA series that is the most bitter he's done. The camera pitches and yaws as if Robert had become unbalanced or been caught in an earthquake (pls. 29 and 30). Such pictures epitomize that despair from which he needed the tonic of Ansel's work to recover.[4]

Although Ansel encouraged Robert not "to underestimate ... your work," he may never have seen that work himself since it represented a current trend he didn't appreciate. "I find it very difficult," his letter confessed, "to comprehend much of the ... art expression of our era." Whether Ansel knew Robert's work or not, Robert's admiration for Ansel was sincere and knowledgeable. Not mentioned in Robert's letter was the first book he had published, in 1970, *White Churches of the Plains*, which had been inspired by the first photograph he'd ever bought, a print of Ansel's most famous image, "Moonrise, Hernandez, New Mexico."

The relationship between the two Adamses is characteristic of a larger historical dialectic that developed in West Coast landscape photography between the 1940s and the 1980s. Though their attitude was not usually reciprocated, the later generation represented by Robert Adams, Lewis Baltz, Joe Deal and others in the 1975 exhibition *New Topographics: Photographs of a Man-Altered Landscape*, tried to appreciate the earlier generation of Ansel Adams, Edward Weston, Minor White and their followers. Yet the younger photographers had an ambivalence about their elders and the Modernist tradition in landscape photography inherited from them.

In order to trace this complex development as it played out in Southern California—this seismic shift in Western landscape photography from the northern part of the state to the southern—I want to follow it more or less chronologically from the period when Weston and Ansel Adams were the unchallenged masters in this genre to the point 40 years later, when Robert Adams, Baltz, Deal, and others working in the LA region known as SoCal were challenging and in some ways undermining the authority of that earlier precedent in landscape.

Colin Westerbeck was Director of the University of California, Riverside/ California Museum of Photography from 2008 until 2011.

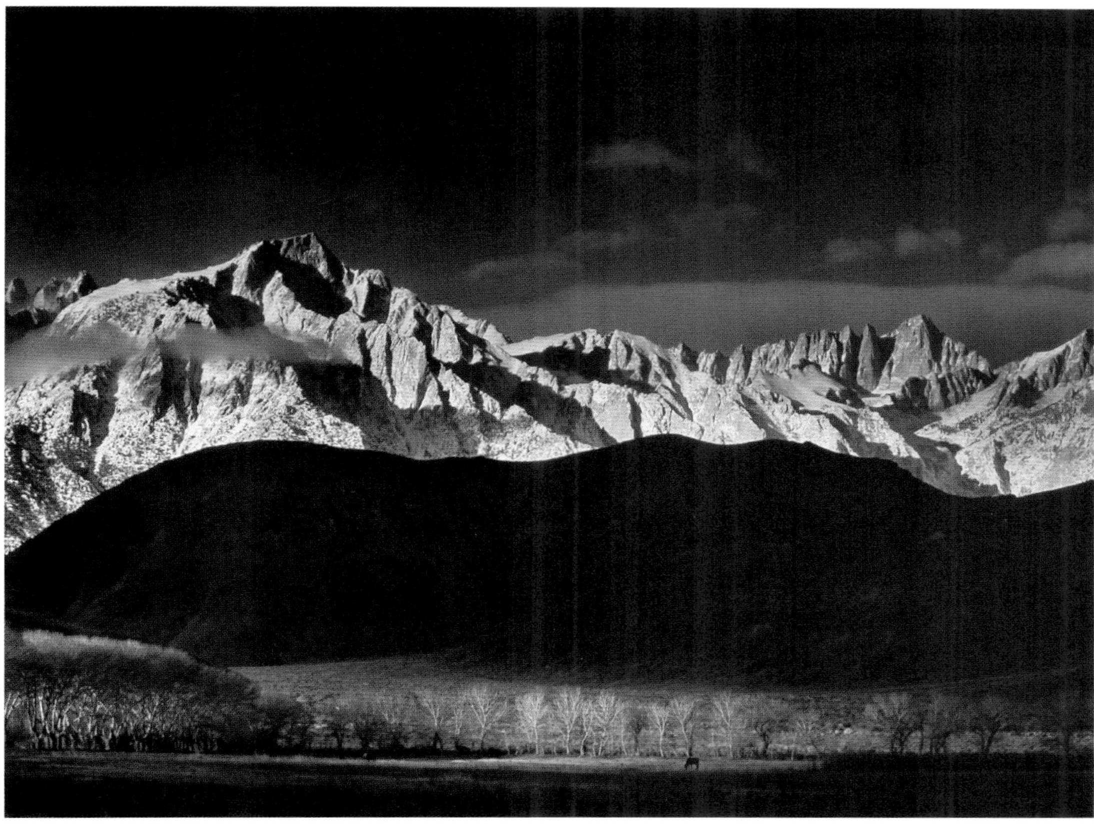

FIGURE 1. **Ansel Adams**, Winter Sunrise, Sierra Nevada, from Lone Pine, California, 1944 (printed 1980), UCR/California Museum of Photography

Ansel Adams, Edward Weston, and the Tradition

The print that Robert Adams had bought was from a negative Ansel made in 1941 as America's involvement in the War loomed. The date of that negative was October 31, slightly more than a month before Pearl Harbor, and that picture and two he would make in 1944 as the War began to enter its final phase, "Winter Sunrise, The Sierra Nevada, from Lone Pine, California" and "Mount Williamson, Sierra Nevada, from Manzanar, California," comprise perhaps his most iconic work ever. It is striking that these images were not created in Yosemite, the national park with which he is associated, but in the countryside; they depict nature as sheltering, rather than being free from, human culture.

At the time he made "Moonrise, Hernandez," Adams also had projects originating in New York and Washington, D. C., and shuttling back and forth between the coasts caused him to lead a more cosmopolitan life than ever before. Opportunities he'd accepted—a commission from Interior Secretary Harold Ickes to create photo murals for government buildings, appointment to the photography committee for the newly formed department at the Museum of Modern Art, and a photographic exhibition he proposed, *The Image of Freedom*, co-curated by him and the museum's top administrators—all entailed responsibilities with a cross-country reach and a national, even patriotic purpose. The effect was to lift his sense of his own photography to a new, epic level.

Adams believed his photography, as his biographer Jonathan Spaulding put it, "contributed to the War effort by presenting the landscape of America and the values it embodied."[5] This last phrase is key as Adams did indeed believe that the values his photographs reveal existed out there, in nature—or rather, Nature—itself. Moreover, "Moonrise, Hernandez" and "Winter Sunrise, Lone Pine" both entailed moments of do-or-die drama appropriate to the atmosphere of national crisis. The light effects that make those two pictures succeed required split-second timing captured on a single negative, without which all would have been lost.

Because of the way that they play the foreground off against the background, "Winter Sunrise, Lone Pine" and "Mount Williamson" also express flawlessly Adams's abiding Transcendentalism—his faith, handed down from his New England forebears and writ large in the Western landscape, that the microcosm near at hand and the macrocosm seen from afar reflect one another. Thus does the dark horse in the sunlit field mimic the foothills in shadow seen against the mountain majesty beyond. So, too, do the boulders in sharp focus scattered at Adams's feet stand up against Mount Williamson, shrouded in radiant mist miles away.

Having evolved from a fuzzy-focused Pictorialist into a sharp-eyed Modernist, Adams had been a founder of Group f.64, a collective of West Coast photographers dedicated to the clarity and depth of field that only the smallest aperture setting on the lens (f.64) could provide. This was Modernism at its most messianic and evangelical, an adamantine faith in modern art as the road to salvation in a beautiful but hard, cold world. The "philosophy of Group f.64" was, Adams admitted, "Calvinistic."[6] No Adams image expresses the uniquely American Romanticism inherent in such a world view better than "Mount Williamson." Through such photographs, the intensity of Adams's personal journey, synchronized with the global crisis of the War, was preparing him to be the public figure and national spokesman he became after 1945.

At the same time, ironically, Edward Weston, Adams's most prominent colleague in f.64, was in decline. Weston had always lived an artistic life in stark contrast to Adams's. Weston and his muse, Charis Wilson, had in recent years settled into a spartan, bohemian, secluded, almost reclusive life on Wildcat Hill near Point Lobos. Moreover, by the mid-1940s, he was in the early stages of Parkinson's disease, which would end his photographic career in 1948, just as Adams was on his way to becoming a celebrity artist. Yet it was Weston, more than Adams, who affected postwar photography in California. From Minor White in the late 1940s to, surprisingly, Lewis Baltz in the late 1960s (see Baltz excerpt, p. 21), Weston was the predominant influence.

Minor White and the Transformation of the Tradition

The teaching career Adams began in LA continued in San Francisco. In 1946, he set up the photography program at the California School of Fine Arts (CSFA). But before the year was out, he'd received a Guggenheim fellowship and was looking for a replacement. Minor White, who came to CSFA as a student in the summer, wound up taking over Adams's teaching duties in the fall. Adams concurred in the choice of this precocious newcomer despite recognizing that White's approach was very different from his. "It was the inner message of the photograph that most concerned him," Adams observed, "to know the thoughts, feelings and reactions of the artist."[7]

Whereas Adams's activities on the homefront during the War had invigorated him, White's service in the military had had the opposite effect. Awaiting induction, he'd photographed a squirrel hit by a truck, commenting, "This is what war means. That smashed

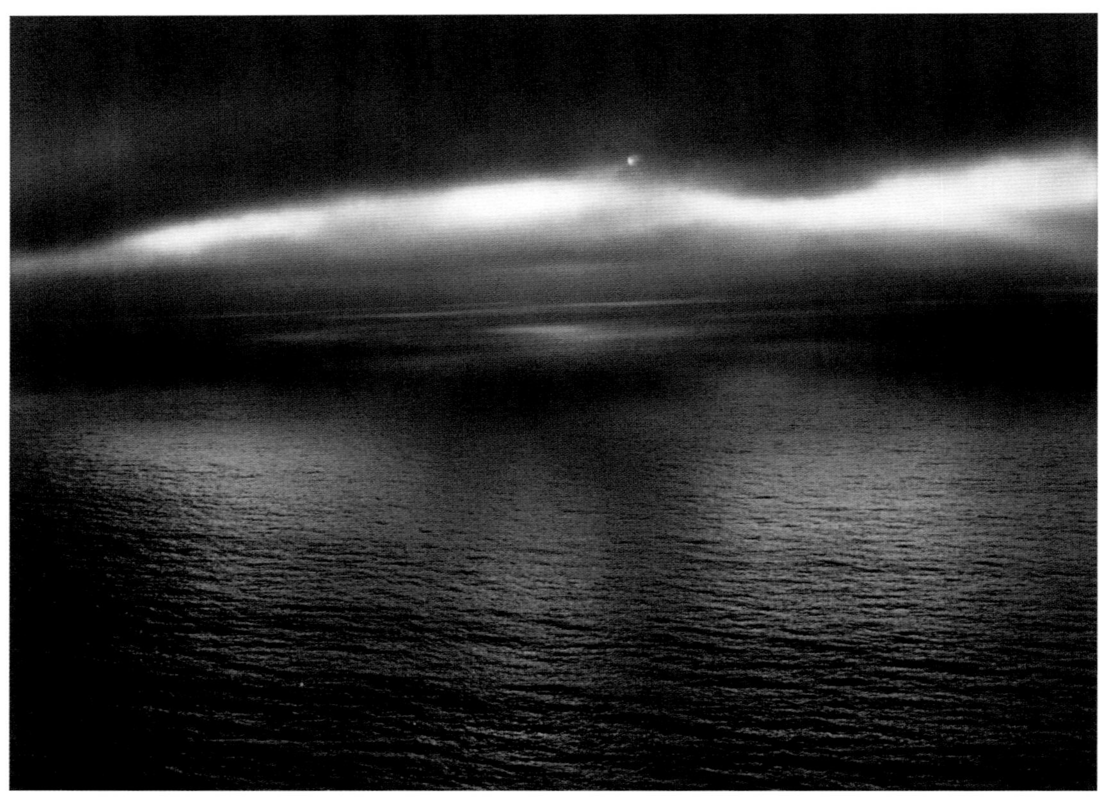

FIGURE 2. **Minor White**, Devil's Slide, San Mateo County, California, 1947 (printed 1975), Los Angeles County Museum of Art

animal just got caught."[8] After the War, a photographic and poetic meditation on his experiences entitled *Amputations*, having been scheduled as an exhibition at San Francisco's Legion of Honor, was then cancelled by the museum because White's poems about comrades lost in battle dwelled on private feelings and expressed his own disillusionment with patriotism.[9] In part, the anguish White experienced in the war was due to his homosexuality, which he had to keep secret in the 24th Infantry but had acknowledged to his parents when a teenager.[10]

After the mass displacement of the Depression ("the Army of the Unemployed") and mass conscription of World War II, many Americans felt a need for individuation in their lives. White's emphasis on photography as a means of self-expression rather than social documentation struck a chord with his postwar students, especially those coming to art school on the GI Bill. White's disposition was also why Weston's solitary devotion to photography appealed to him more than Adams's public persona. According to Peter Bunnell, Weston had "the most profound effect on White of any artist."[11] In November 1946, White made a pilgrimage to Point Lobos to meet Weston, whom he visited repeatedly with his students thereafter. His class in "Subjective Photography" made a field trip to Carmel the next summer. Weston and White were an odd couple in photography, but the former's aesthetic appealed to the latter in ways that transcended differences in sensibility.

Inspired by Weston's absorption in Point Lobos (pls. 5 and 8), White's photography shifted the focus of West Coast landscape from the mountains to the sea (fig. 2). The roiling emotions he needed his photography to express found an ideal vehicle in the ocean's paradox of being eternal, yet ever changing. "This morning at Lobos I started out by saying to myself, 'What will I be given today?'," White wrote while working on a series called *Sequence 8*, "Watching moving water was, and always is, mesmeric."[12] A 1951 picture from *Sequence 8*, "Point Lobos State Park" (pl. 7), demonstrates his tendency to ground with a place name the disorienting symbolism in his pictures. The relationship of foreground to background that makes an Adams photograph orderly is foreshortened in White's to a point that sows confusion. The solidity of rock striped with bird lime in his foreground dissolves in the foamy surf beyond, thereby creating an Abstract Expressionist composition.

In a 1947 handmade book of White's entitled *Song Without Words*, another surf photograph is seen not in this subject's conventional orientation, which is horizontal, but as a vertical (pl. 9). A necessary accommodation because the page is vertical, his placement is nonetheless radical in effect, causing us to see the image as suggestive rather than descriptive. Formally, the vertical line of surf pairs with the photograph of a narrow inlet on the facing page. But seen vertically, the surf also takes on a phallic shape and a new connotation next to the attractive young male sprawled on the rocks in the foreground on the opposite page. In 1964 in the magazine he'd founded, *Aperture*, White wrote, "To the photographer temperamentally compelled to work inwardly his medium forces him to use the outward landscape to manifest by way of metaphor the inner reality."[13] He was compelled to work "inwardly" not by inclination alone, but also by the times in which he lived, forcing him to keep his homosexual feelings an "inner reality" that he could express only obliquely in his landscapes.

Beyond the direct impact that his photographs or teaching may have had, White's philosophy seems to have shaped California landscape photography in a general way during the period following his 1954 departure from the West Coast. His aura was suffused through the photography of the next couple of decades, spreading less like a direct influence than one of the mystical experiences in which he believed. Wynn Bullock, who was born in 1902 (the same year as Ansel Adams), had absorbed White's lessons *avant la lettre*, and among members of the Visual Dialogue Foundation (VDF), a Bay Area group that flourished from 1968 until 1972, the sprit of Minor White lived on. His inspiration touched the younger photographers in the VDF like Don Worth, Oliver Gagliani, Michael Bishop, and Thomas Algernon Weir. Despite differences between White's views and Adams's, White extended the tradition of Adams and Weston by transforming it into an aesthetic adapted to the existential age of the postwar era.

From Wynn Bullock to the Visual Dialogue Foundation

The most direct descendant of Weston was, of course, his son Brett (pls. 11 and 12), who first showed his work with his father's at age 15, in 1927, and who, with the rise of the photography market 50 years later, would become something his father never dreamed of being—a millionaire.[14] In the military en route to a new base assignment at the end of 1945, Brett discovered New Mexico's White Sands National Monument.[15] The result was the publication of a 1949 portfolio that made sand dunes, whose study he would continue at Oceano, California and elsewhere, into a subject of endless fascination for him just as Point Lobos had been for his father (fig. 3). His talk, like his photography, was straight. He denounced "Minor's theories" as something that "just bores the hell out of me" and condemned photography "mongrelized by . . . bizarre retouching and alteration."[16] He attacked White personally, perhaps, because he realized White's theories were increasingly being used to license such manipulation.

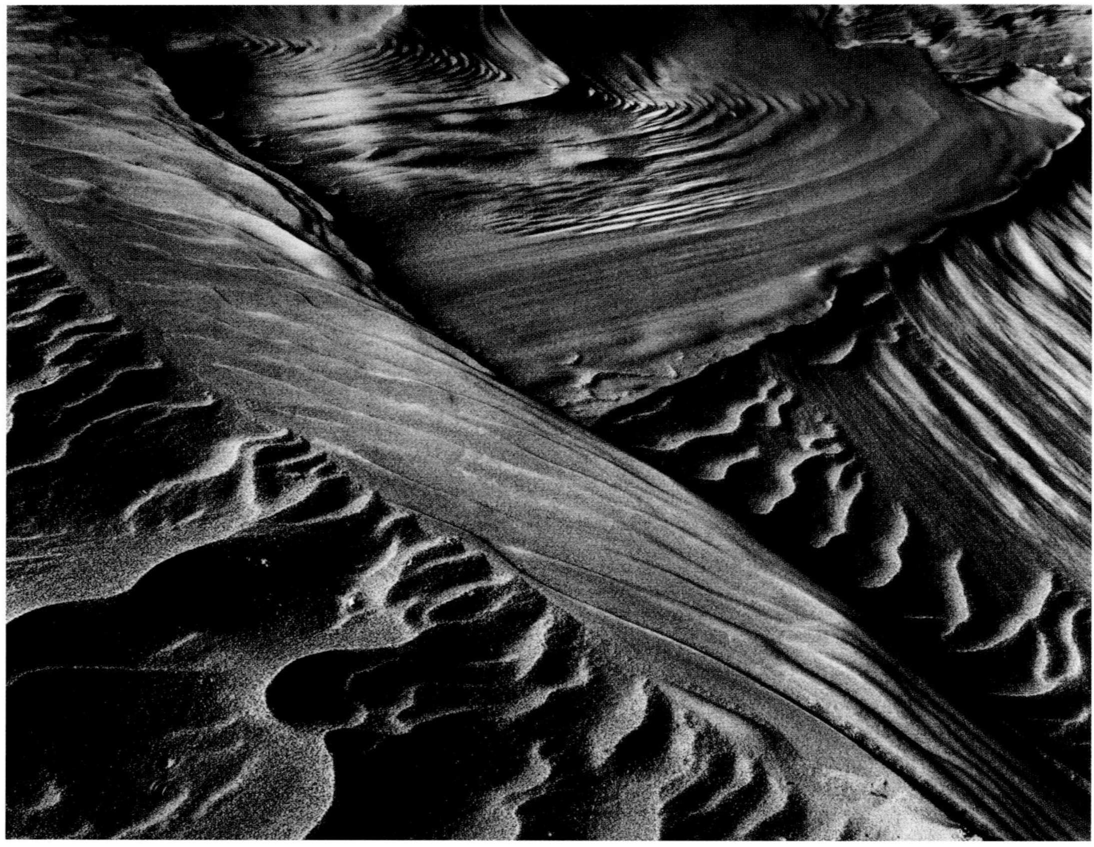

FIGURE 3. **Brett Weston**, Dunes, Baja, 1967, Collection of Amy Harrison

Wynn Bullock's photography paralleled and even anticipated White's (pl. 13). He studied at LA's Art Center School between 1938 and 1940, just before Adams's tenure there, when teacher Edward Kaminski encouraged the very un-Adams techniques of altering negatives before printing by scratching, cutting, collaging, or smearing them with ink.[17] Within the decade, Bullock had met Weston, whose penchant for nudes as well as landscapes, and nudes in landscapes, he shared. While Weston's precedent persuaded Bullock for a while to abandon manipulative technique, Bullock soon gave up the purist Modernism of the straight print for an eclectic approach. His 1956 "Twin Oaks" (fig. 4), for example, contains at least three collaged negatives. His loyalty to Weston's vision of nature coupled with a return to Kaminski's interventions was based on his new-found principle that "opposites are one."[18]

Like Adams, Bullock was capable of making iconic pictures with mass appeal; a moonlit seascape of his was voted the most popular photograph in the 1955 blockbuster exhibition *The Family of Man* at its Washington venue.[19] But just as White was attracted to esoteric philosophers like Gurdjieff, so was Bullock influenced by Alfred Korzybski, whose book on "Non-Aristotelian Systems" helped the photographer transcend Weston's hold on his imagination. Like White, too, Bullock changed the orientation of some images (he turned them upside down). In his 1968 "Girl on Beach" (pl. 18), a nude sits in the lotus position as she contemplates an encroaching tide that appears to have trapped her in a cove. The picture up-dated for the counter-culture of the sixties beliefs of Bullock's that were aligned with Minor White's. The year of this picture, 1968, was when the VDF was started, also in response to the way the times they were a-changin'.

VDF was organized by students at San Francisco State College (SFSC) and inspired by the teaching there of Don Worth and Jack Welpott, whose interest in Carl Jung's writings on dreams and symbolism matched White's.[20] Worth had been an assistant to Ansel Adams from 1956 until 1960, and his relationship with Adams had another dimension characteristic of landscape photographers in this phase of the genre's history. Adams had considered a career as a concert pianist before coming to photography, and so had Worth, who studied at Julliard.[21] VDF member Oliver Gagliani, who had studied with Adams and White, originally intended to be a composer.[22] (pl. 17) And Bullock, who taught briefly at San Francisco State, had been a professional singer for a decade before coming to photography.[23] White had struck a familiar chord when he titled his early photographic book *Song Without Words*.

Romanticism was kept alive in this generation of photographers by that tradition in music as much as in the visual arts.

Bullock's influence was apparent in the work of at least one student and VDF member, Michael Bishop, who inverted prints as Bullock had.[24] Another member, Harvey Himmelfarb, followed White's lead with a series called *Vertical Landscapes*.[25] The bond among the VDF members was summed up by Leland Rice in terms that take us right back to White's precedent. "These photographers attempt to externalize their psychological relationship to nature," Rice said, adding that "the key to the photographer is his search for self-discovery."[26] But the VDF was also transforming yet again what White had already transformed in the tradition going back to Weston and Adams. The VDF work pushed the apparitional qualities of White's landscapes from the 1940s and 1950s toward the hallucinogenic in the 1960s. Photographic historian Darwin Marable summed up the situation when he wrote that "to live in the San Francisco Bay Area during the sixties, one could not help but be influenced by the quest for self-discovery attempted through encounter groups, meditation, psychotherapy, and LSD, and these consciousness-raising techniques impacted . . . the imagery of the VDF."[27]

Some reciprocity existed between the dynamic San Francisco group and the more scattered LA photography scene. One of three dinners VDF hosted to honor older photographers was for LA-based Edmund Teske, whose unique duotone solarizations (pls. 2 and 14) epitomized the highly personal expression to which VDF members aspired. Likewise, a VDF exhibition held at the Friends of Photography in Carmel in the winter of 1972 traveled that spring to the Pasadena Museum of Art. In the exhibition's catalogue, Jack Welpott quoted Edward Weston's contention that American photography expresses "an epoch, a race in the making, the becoming," and he claimed that the VDF photographers in the exhibition were "the new wave of the epoch referred to. . . . They are 'the becoming.'" But the Pasadena venue was to be the final one for the VDF's last show before the group disbanded.

Fred R. Parker and Rumblings in SoCal

Despite having been Welpott's student at SFSC, the curator at Pasadena who brought the Carmel show there, Fred R. Parker, had done two shows of his own suggesting Southern California photographers were moving away from the Northern aesthetic. In his catalogue for *California Photographers 1970*, he said the assumption that Weston and Adams were the photographers who "would continue to be the most . . . exemplary for further generations . . . does not reflect the total current situation."[28] While noting ways that "the Point Lobos of Weston is being

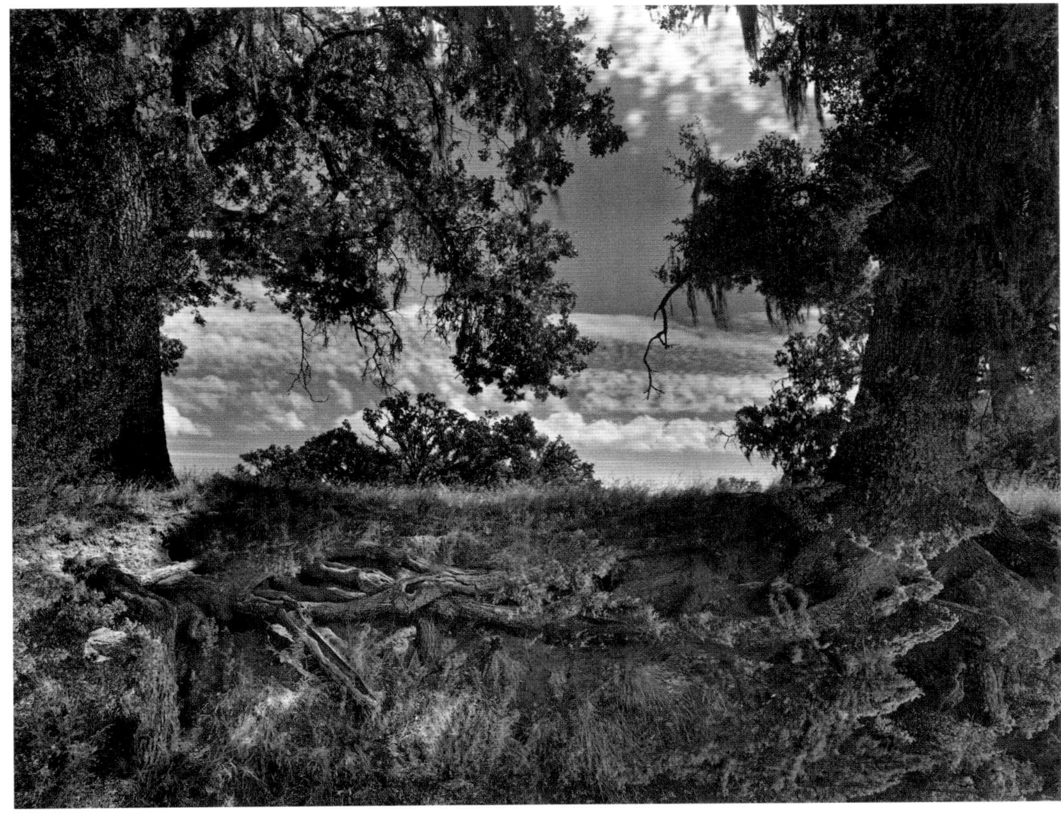

FIGURE 4. **Wynn Bullock**, Twin Oaks, 1956, UCR/California Museum of Photography

expanded with psychedelic vision," Parker included in his exhibition work that was not only unmanipulated, but obdurate in the way that it presented flat, commonplace subject matter in equally flat, unmodulated light. Having begun his plate section with a tripped-out image by Todd Walker, Parker pointedly ended it with a head-on photograph of a typical California picture window with its blinds drawn—an image credited to C. Lewis Baltz.

Most of the pictures on the map Parker's exhibition drew were, nonetheless, heavily manipulated, thereby prompting an *LA Times* headline branding the show a "Study in Poetic Exhaustion."[29] Parker devoted his next show, *The Crowded Vacancy*, solely to photographers who worked in the new, self-erasing style: Terry Wild, Anthony Hernandez and, again, Lewis Baltz (he'd now dropped his first initial). Even in the VDF show Parker brought to Pasadena, there were signs of defection. While one print by Oliver Gagliani in the Friends of Photography catalogue contains nine inset negatives superimposed on a tenth in classic VDF style, his other reproduction, of broken windows set into a raw plywood wall, could have been in *The Crowded Vacancy*. The fact is that even in the work of older traditionalists like Bullock and Brett Weston, ambiguities emerged, as they did in the photography of Leland Rice (pls. 21, 22 and 23)

Lewis Baltz and Joe Deal, from the UCR/California Museum of Photography to the New Topographics

In 1973, Rice and Baltz came together in an exhibition, not as exhibitors of their own work, but as lenders of historical photography from their personal collections. Held at the University of California, Riverside (UCR), to celebrate the university's newly founded California Museum of Photography, the exhibition was entitled *Revolution in a Box* because it displayed cameras along with prints. Behind the exhibition was an Assistant Dean of the Arts, Ed Beardsley, who wanted the show to honor a local collector's donation of the cameras and commissioned as curator a recent Pomona College graduate with a degree in "perceptual psychology." The curator was James Turrell, through whom Baltz got involved because he was then teaching at Pomona.[30]

If the California landscape photography of the last couple of decades inspired by White, with its self-involvement and tendency to let its increasingly crude darkroom technique show, was a response to Abstract Expressionism, Turrell's art and Baltz's were both spin-offs of Minimalism, albeit going in opposite directions. Turrell would further reduce the seemingly irreducible values of Minimalist painting by doing away even with paint and canvas, transforming color field imagery into an immaterial scrim of pure light. Baltz made Minimalist imagery more concrete, literally, by photographing in black and white the bare walls of industrial buildings and tract housing under construction. Putting their two heads together with Rice's at the UCR's California Museum of Photography for the inaugural exhibition made it into a provocative essay on the history of the medium.

In a "Sketch" of photographic history that Rice wrote for the catalogue, there is an entry on the 19th-century Western landscapes by Timothy O'Sullivan and William Henry Jackson. Dissatisfied with recent landscape photography, Baltz and other newcomers were reaching back over the 20th-century history of art photography to re-discover the 19th-century precedent in landscape provided by O'Sullivan. Having come into being as contract work for government-sponsored geological and topographical surveys of the West, photography by O'Sullivan and others appealed to these young photographers because it didn't idealize nature. Some more recent landscapes by contemporary commercial photographer William Garnett also revealed how mixed emotions—or mixed motivations, anyway—were seeping into this genre.

Garnett's unique postwar career in aerial photography landed him a commission from the developers of Lakewood, at the time the largest housing tract ever built in LA, to create for promotional purposes views of the new homes under construction. But then the same photographs were reproduced by Ansel Adams in his 1960 polemic *This Is the American Earth* to illustrate his contention that LA had become "Hell . . . on earth," and these pictures appeared again four years later in Peter Blake's book *God's Own Junkyard*, whose title speaks for itself. In the year that the Adams book came out, the first model homes opened on an 8,000-acre tract of Brea Canyon in Diamond Bar where Transamerica Corp. would soon build housing for 50,000 people.[31] While continuing his commercial career, Garnett also did personal work whose scenic beauty was inspired by Adams. But at the same time, he couldn't help noticing from the air, and documenting, desecrations of the landscape like the bulldozing of a walnut grove or a leaking sewage tank (pl. 10.).[32]

The seminal influence that Baltz was having by the early 1970s is seen in the work of Laurie Brown, who would do pioneering photographs of "terraforming," the massive bulldozing of a landscape to make it a scenic setting for a new development (pl. 26). Brown says that, "though I only took one class from Lewis Baltz, he is the individual whose work . . . influenced me the most."[33] According to an academic paper Brown wrote in 1973 after interviewing him, Baltz, who haled from Newport Beach, enrolled in 1964 at Monterey Peninsula College because it was near where Wynn Bullock lived in Carmel.[34] "My photographic style at this time," Baltz told Brown, "was concerned with . . . symbolic mysticism."

But in 1967, while photographing at Point Lobos, he came to feel that "to express my profound feelings and emotions in this way rendered them trivial or trite, and I saw it as a boring self-indulgence. . . . I began to notice the world I was participating in on a daily basis (parking lots, surface streets, etc.). . . . At this point I began photographing common objects." [35]

When Bullock proved unresponsive to the new direction in his work, Baltz looked elsewhere for guidance. Finding it at the Claremont Graduate School, he began his *Tract Houses* series as his MA thesis and received encouragement from one of his professors, Hal Glicksman. When William Jenkins, an Assistant Curator from George Eastman House in Rochester (GEH), came through LA and looked Baltz up, because the two had met on a 1971 Baltz visit to GEH, Baltz introduced Jenkins to Glicksman, and the three of them brainstormed an idea Jenkins had for a show on photography of architecture. As Baltz and Jenkins discussed other young photographers they knew doing work similar to Baltz's, the exhibition plans expanded to include everything in this specialty from the 19th century to Baltz and his contemporaries.[36]

One young photographer Baltz and Jenkins both thought of was Joe Deal, who had come to George Eastman House in 1971 to be a museum guard, his alternative service as a Conscientious Objector to the Vietnam War. Jenkins realized that Deal was underemployed, so when Baltz came to show his photographs Jenkins invited Deal to look at them too. "I think you'll like them," Jenkins told Deal, and so a friendship between Baltz and Deal developed that would grow over the next few years whenever Deal got to LA. The relationship flourished, Deal felt, because "We were both looking for something that we couldn't put our fingers on in photographs that had to be kind of cool, distant, with a clear and hard view of the world—an unromantic and unfiltered way of looking through the lens."[37] (pls. 32 and 43)

Discussions about the architecture exhibition lasted a couple of years. On his return from LA, Jenkins reported the conversation he'd had there to Deal, with whom he'd talked about the exhibition before his trip. When the subject came up a year or so later during a planning meeting at GEH, Deal had an insight that Jenkins and Baltz thought profound. The exhibition's subject was not really architecture, Deal argued; it was landscape.[38] In effect, the proposition was that the natural landscape as envisioned by earlier generations of photographers was now blocked from view by the tract housing, strip malls and industrial buildings in the foreground. These features *were* the landscape now. In the interim between his initial talks with Jenkins and his perceptive analysis of the concept for the exhibition, Deal's own career in photography had advanced. This personal development was what led him to his insight.

His earlier photographs of period buildings around Rochester had gotten Jenkins thinking about architecture as a subject, but while Deal was on leave from GEH during the academic year 1973–74, earning an MA in photography at the University of New Mexico, his point of view as a photographer changed. Asked to make a photograph for a an architecture department poster, Deal happened upon a housing development that backed up against a hill on Albuquerque's outskirts, so he climbed up to get a better view. "I grew up in the suburbs and I wanted to photograph what I knew. . . . I stood up on a hillside and looked down on Albuquerque, and it just startled me that here, spread before me, was what I'd been looking for. . . . I wanted to photograph the landscape, and the buildings became part of the landscape."[39]

As if anticipating the fuss such photographs were to cause, Deal added, "I had no intention of turning my back on California landscape photography traditions." Nonetheless, that was the effect of the new point of view he and Baltz were taking. Whereas Adams had taken the long view, stretching the focus from near foreground to remote background, Baltz and Deal were taking an immediate view. Though inspired by Weston, White had intensified the view Adams took to near the breaking point where background and foreground were telescoped until the distinction between them almost collapsed. Though it may not have been their intent, Baltz and Deal overthrew this entire historic progression by finding a point of view that was completely and unmistakably flat.

Like Baltz's photographs of the interior walls of tract houses and exteriors of warehouses, Deal's top-down view of the suburban landscape usually eliminated the horizon line that gave viewers their bearings in earlier work and used the sky to dramatize the landscape. Thus did the two photographers make the vast, open spaces of the Western landscape in earlier photography alarmingly claustrophobic. Their photography documented, truly, the closing of the frontier. The earth was now flat—at least, in SoCal. The new work was what would be called a paradigm shift today, an historical moment when the received wisdom isn't refined or refreshed, but contradicted.

With Deal in the graduate program at Albuquerque was Nick Nixon, whose friends from back East, Frank Gohlke (pl. 27) and John Schott, would come to town occasionally. The four of them plus Baltz were among the photographers included in the exhibition Jenkins finally pulled together after Deal had returned to GEH with the new position of director of exhibitions. Opening at GEH in October 1975, *New Topographics* was more modest in scope than originally planned. It had lost its historical perspective and become an exhibition of contemporary landscape only. Each of the nine photographers (counting Hilla and Bernd Becher as one) had 20 prints in the exhibition, but only three reproductions in the 50-page catalogue. Even so, the catalogue was what spread the word, because few people saw the exhibition at its three venues. Its lone West Coast venue of only one month was LA's Otis Art Institute, where Hal Glicksman had been appointed director of the art gallery in 1975.[40] Despite the modesty of both exhibition and catalogue, it had a tremendous impact that continues to influence landscape photography today.[41]

Besides Deal and Baltz, the one other California photographer in the exhibition was Henry Wessel (pls. 28 and 41), who had enrolled at Rochester's Visual Studies Workshop in 1969 at the same time as Jenkins and another curator, Dennis Longwell. It was to escape the grim winter there that Wessel first visited LA. When he walked out of the airport, he has said, "The light had such a physical presence; it looked as though you could lean against it."[42] Although he has made his home in San Francisco since 1971, Wessel has returned often to Southern California, attracted, Longwell has claimed, by LA's "peculiar juxtaposition of vast nothingness and clutter."[43] Unlike Wessel's San Francisco pictures, streaked with long, melancholy shadows or made after nightfall, the light in the SoCal work is insidious and all-pervasive.

The first time Wessel visited New York's Museum of Modern Art to show his work, the director of the photography department, John Szarkowski, got out photographs for him to look at by novelist Wright Morris, whom Szarkowski thought of as a kindred spirit to Wessel. Wessel became so absorbed by Morris's writing as well as his photographs that, unable to locate a building whose picture Morris had included in his photographic book, *The Inhabitants*, Wessel wrote Morris a letter about it.[44] Baltz is a fan of *The Inhabitants*, too, and of Morris as both writer and photographer.[45] Whereas two earlier generations of landscape photographers had in common their love of music, as noted above, this generation has had a literary bent. Robert Adams was a professor of English before turning to photography, and Gohlke originally studied literature.[46]

The one California photographer Jenkins has said he regrets not including in his show is the LA painter Ed Ruscha, whose little photographic books like *Thirtyfour Parking Lots in Los Angeles* (1967) impressed Baltz, Deal and Robert Adams.[47] Opinions were mixed among these photographers, however. While Baltz felt Ruscha's books gave him an idea of how to achieve a "photography degree zero," Robert Adams described them with faint deprecation as "clever, sometimes funny."[48] It was this quality in the books that put off Deal. In his own photography, he wanted to "find a different way of photographing . . . subject matter that wouldn't satirize it."[49] In Ruscha's work, Deal deplored "the way he exploits [his subjects]—and exploit I think is the right word. What makes him different from the New Topographic photographers is that he has an Oscar Wilde sense of humor, making life art."[50] Robert Adams concurred when he said, "Fundamentally, I think we need to discover a non-ironic world."[51]

For Baltz and Deal, the way to give their photography the gravitas Adams sought was to work serially. Among the standards they were rejecting was the ideal of the masterpiece, like Ansel Adams's "Moonrise, Hernandez" or "Mt. Williamson." The 20 Baltz photographs in *New Topographics* at GEH were all from his 1974 series *New Industrial Parks near Irvine, California* (pls. 33, 45, 49 and 50), and the Deal work included was from his year in Albuquerque. Because he was criticized for being in an exhibition he had helped curate, Deal realized he must find a means of support that wouldn't compromise his photography. When Ed Beardsley offered him a job in 1976 teaching photography at UCR, Deal accepted and later that year began a California series, *The Fault Zone* (pls. 3, 25, and 39). While Deal would continue to make new series throughout his career, Baltz drew a line under this American phase of his work when he moved to Paris in the late 1980s.

But before moving on, Baltz was back on the UCR campus in 1983, this time teaching a seminar whose purpose was to produce a portfolio to which everyone in the class would contribute. The result was a series done by many hands. Among the "students" were a number of UCR staff and faculty, including a visiting professor, the distinguished photographic historian Helmut Gernsheim. Almost all the work has a very New Topographical look. Adjunct Lecturer Herb Quick contributed a photograph of an Orange County industrial building that looks more like a Baltz than Baltz's own photograph. And Joe Deal was in the mix too, with a good example of his own work at that time (fig. 5). The portfolio, entitled *Sideviews* (pls. 4 and 47), is a real time capsule, not least because it represents the last time Baltz and Deal would work in tandem as they had on *New Topograhics*.

Conclusion

There's a California photography collector who, having made his money in real estate, likes to acquire pictures containing property that "could be owned or leased." This is a taste with a distinguished history, for as Deborah Bright has pointed out in an essay on cultural meaning in landscape photography, "'natural' landscape that celebrated property ownership" goes back to the rise of the merchant class in 17th-century Holland.[52] Suburban development and the profit motive that drives it impose an abstraction on the land for which the way has been

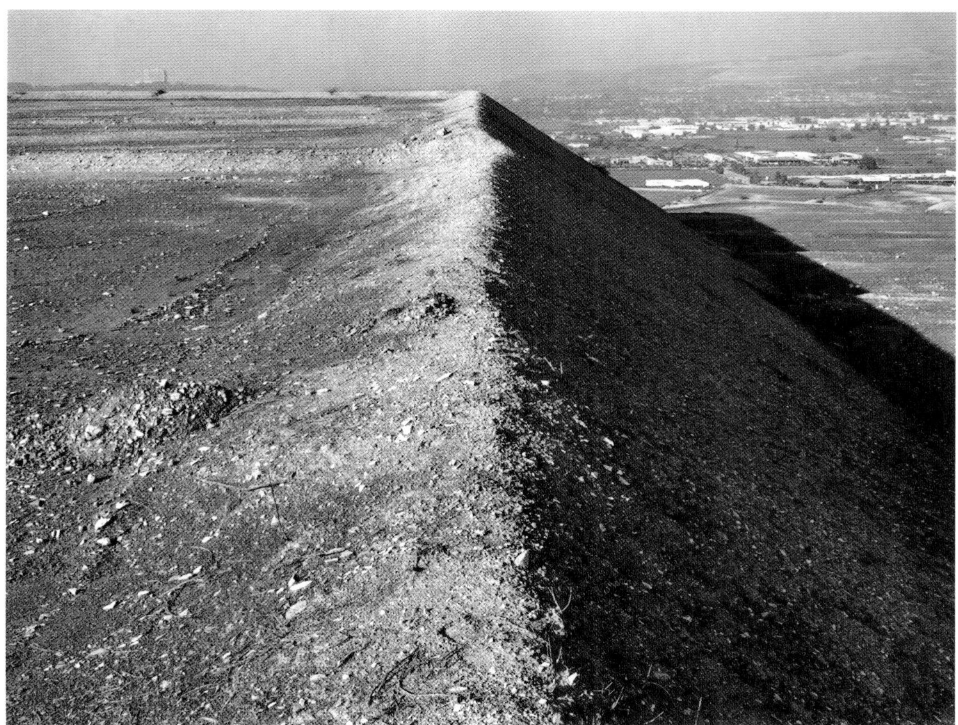

FIGURE 5. **Joe Deal**, Puente Hills, California, 1983, *Sideviews* portfolio, UCR/California Museum of Photography

paved in SoCal by another kind of abstraction, the grid system of our streets. In the West, especially, this is the ultimate refinement of the way boundaries were established by the Northwest Ordinance of 1787, a "triumph of geometry over topography," as landscape historian J. B. Jackson put it.[53]

Robert Adams's photography is the most sensitive to the way that the abstract geometry of straight lines, in the form of road construction, guard rails, the zip strip of neon lighting, the blockiness of tract housing, etc., cuts through and cuts off the irregular, accommodating, biomorphic shapes that nature takes. In the late 1960s, emerging New Topograhical work like Adams's was anathema in San Francisco's democratic anarchy of art. In 1961, CSFA, where Ansel Adams and Minor White had taught, was renamed the San Francisco Art Institute. There, according to Bill Arnold, an "idealistic photo movement" soon developed that "was officially strangled in 1975 with *New Topographics*."[54] This goes too far, though. The history is more ambiguous than that. (After all, Baltz got his BFA at San Francisco Art Institute too, in 1969.)

A more just term would be one used at the beginning of this essay to describe Robert Adams's attitude toward Ansel Adams: ambivalence. Baltz used the term himself in a 1975 *Art in America* review of Robert Adams's book *The New West*, finding a "sense of ambivalence in many [Adams] photographs."[55] Despite the letter in which Robert told Ansel that his photographs "have rescued me often from my own despair," in the opening essay of his 1981 book *Beauty in Photography* Robert wrote as if he was speaking again to Ansel and now having second thoughts about what he saw in Ansel's photographs. "Scenic grandeur is today sometimes painful," Robert admitted. "The beautiful places to which we journey for inspiration surprise us by the melancholy they can induce. . . . Unspoiled places sadden us because they are, in an important sense, no longer true."[56] The truth lay now in a landscape that had been overrun by development and obscured from view, until the New Topographics brought it to our attention.

Notes

1 Robert Adams's letter dated June 26, 1979 and Ansel's misdated reply are reproduced in Adam D. Weinberg, et al., *Reinventing the West: The Photographs of Ansel Adams and Robert Adams* (Andover, MA: Addison Gallery of American Art, Phillips Academy, 2001): 10.

2 Jonathan Spaulding, *Ansel Adams and the American Landscape* (Berkeley: University of California Press, 1995): 171–72 and 199–200. See also Jennifer A. Watts, Moving in Place: Los Angeles in Photographs, in Watts, et al., *This Side of Paradise: Body and landscape in Los Angeles Photographs* (New York: Merrell, 2008): 58.

3 Ansel Adams and Nancy Newhall, *This is the American Earth* (San Francisco: Sierra Club, 1960): 36

4 Robert Adams's LA series was published as *Los Angeles Spring* (Millerton, NY: Aperture, 1986).

5 Spaulding (1995): 193.

6 *Ansel Adams: An Autobiography* (Boston: Little, Brown and Co., 1985): 320.

7 *Ansel Adams: An Autobiography* (1985): 318.
8 Isabel Kane Bradley, Minor in La Grande, 1940–1941, in *Minor White: A Living Memory* (Millerton, NY: Aperture, 1984): 26
9 Jeff Gunderson's title essay for Stephanie Comer and Deborah Klochko, *Moment of Seeing: Minor White and the California School of Fine Arts* (San Francisco: Chronicle Books, 2006): 36–37.
10 Peter C. Bunnell, *Minor White: The Eye that Shapes* (Princeton: The Princeton University Art Museum, 1989): 1.
11 Bunnell (1989): 5.
12 Minor White, *Mirrors, Messages, Manifestations* (Millerton, NY: Aperture, 1982): 80–81.
13 Quoted in *Minor White: A Living Remembrance* (Millerton, NY: Aperture, 1984): 55.
14 Scott Hale, In His Own Light, in *Weston: Out of the Shadow* (Washington, D.C.: The Phillips Collection, 2008): 1, 41.
15 Hale (2008): 29–30.
16 James Danziger and Barnaby Conrad III, *Interviews with Master Photographers* (New York: Paddington Press, 1977): 167, 171.
17 This is the testimony of photographer Todd Walker, who was also a student at the Art Center School when Bullock was there. See Clyde H. Dilley, *The Photography and Philosophy of Wynn Bullock* (Cranbury, NY: Associated University Presses, 1984): 18.
18 Dilley (1984): 47.
19 Barbara Bullock-Wilson, *Wynn Bullock: Photography, A Way of Life* (Dobbs Ferry, NY: Morgan and Morgan, 1973): 148.
20 Darwin Marable, Visual Dialogue Foundation, *B and W*, issue 16 (December 2001): 59.
21 "A good part of Ansel's immediate interest in me," Worth said, "revolved around our mutual involvement with music." Essay by Leland Rice in *Don Worth: Close to Infinity, Photographs from Six Decades* (Carmel, CA: Photography West Graphics, 2005), unpaged.
22 See the introduction by Leland Rice to *Oliver Gagliani* (Menlo Park, CA: Ideograph, 1975): 12–14.
23 Dilley (1984): 1, 15. Also, Barbara Bullock-Wilson: 9.
24 Marable (2001): 60.
25 Marable (2001): 74.
26 Quoted in Marable (2001): 78.
27 Marable (2001): 64.
28 Fred R. Parker, *California Photographers 1970* (Davis, CA: Memorial Union Art Gallery, University of California, Davis, 1970): 3.
29 William Wilson, Pasadena Shows Are Study in Poetic Exhaustion, *Los Angeles Times*, July 19, 1970.
30 *From 1839: Revolution in a Box—An Historical Survey in Two Parts Presented by the Art Departments of Pomona College and the University of California, Riverside*, 1973, unpaged loose-leaf catalogue.
31 From the website of the City of Diamond Bar (www.ci.diamond-bar.ca.us)
32 Martha A. Sandweiss, *William Garnett, Aerial Photographer* (Los Angeles: University of California Press, 1994): ix.
33 Private communication with the author, September 26, 2010.
34 Laurie Brown, Lewis Baltz–Photographer: A Monograph, unpublished paper submitted to Profs. John Upton and Rick Steadry for a course on "History and Aesthetics of Photography" at Orange Coast College, January 16, 1973: 2. At the time Baltz also gave Brown a copy of a self-interview he had written dated Winter 1972.
35 Quoted in Laurie Brown (1973): 3–5.
36 Among various accounts of this meeting, the most reliable is in Britt Salvesen's introductory essay for *New Topographics: Robert Adams, Lewis Baltz, Bernd and Hilla Becher, Joe Deal, Frank Gohlke, Nicholas Nixon, John Schott, Stephen Shore, Henry Wessel, Jr.* (Tucson, AZ: Center for Creative Photography, and Rochester, NY: George Eastman House, 2009): 18.
37 Unpublished Joe Deal interview with the author, May 13–14, 2010, Providence, RI: 12–13.
38 Deal interview (2010): 16–17.
39 Deal interview (2010): 3–4.
40 The exhibition was seen at the Otis Art Institute not only on a curtailed schedule but with a reduced checklist. See Salvesen (2009): 54.
41 Concurrent with the exhibition *Seismic Shift* at UCR/California Museum of Photography is a second exhibition entitled *Aftershocks* that has in it recent work by three photographers who are also in *Seismic Shift*—Joe Deal, Laurie Brown and John Divola—and three whose careers have emerged since the 1980s—Mark Ruwedel, Michael Light and Brad Moore. All six photographers reflect the continuing legacy of the New Topographics.
42 Henry Wessel, *California and the West* (Göttingen, Germany: Steidel, 2006): 5. James Turrell, whose work was inspired by the same California sunshine, was once threatened with a lawsuit by a woman who tried to lean against one of his light installations, thinking it was solid. James Turrell, lecture delivered at the Getty Museum, Los Angeles, January 11, 2004.
43 From a wall label for the 1972 Wessel exhibition at the Museum of Modern Art, New York, quoted in Sandra Phillips, The Work of Henry Wessel, in *Henry Wessel* (San Francisco: San Francisco Museum of Modern Art, 2007), unpaged.
44 Phillips (2007)l: unpaged.
45 Unpubished Baltz interview by Matthew Witkovsky, November 15, 2009, Paris, France: 4.
46 Salvesen (2009): 22.
47 Salvesen (2009): 27.
48 Adams quoted from a 2007 conversation with Britt Salvesen. See Salvesen (2009): 27 and nt. 82.
49 Joe Deal, interview in *Northlight*, number 4 (May 1977), Arizona State University, Tempe: 3–4.
50 Deal (1977): 10.
51 Robert Adams, interview in *Landscape: Theory* (New York: Lustrum Press, 1980): 6.
52 Deborah Bright, Of Mother Nature and Marlboro Men: An Inquiry into the Cultural Meanings of Landscape Photography, in Richard Bolton, ed., *The Contest of Meaning: Critical Histories of Photography* (Cambridge, MA: MIT Press, 1989): 126–27.
53 John Brinckerhoff Jackson, *Discovering the Vernacular Landscape* (New Haven: Yale University Press, 1984): 16. This book and the journal *Landscape* that Jackson edited have been admired by various New Topographers.
54 Bill Arnold, Photography, a Reflection of the Times, in Gloria Williams Sander, ed., *The Collectible Moment: Catalogue of Photographs in the Norton Simon Museum* (Pasadena, CA: Norton Simon Art Foundation, 2006). p. 100.
55 Reprinted in Thomas F. Barrow, et al, eds., *Reading into Photography: Selected Essays. 1959–1980* (Albuquerque: University of New Mexico Press, 1982): 58.
56 Robert Adams, Truth and Landscape, in *Beauty in Photography: Essays in Defense of Traditional Values* (Millerton, NY: Aperture, 1981): 13–14.

Joe Deal: The project that began in Albuquerque was not really about LA; it was about the West, the photographs that were made in '74. In '77, I got a grant, an NEA Grant, and it gave me enough money just to travel the West. With that grant I photographed in Wyoming and Utah, California up and down, and so, I didn't restrict myself geographically so much in that project. I guess I started *The Fault Zone* around the time I was doing those photographs.

I see it as sort of zeroing in on LA, because after that I made several series of photographs that are about different aspects of Southern California. *The Beach Zone* series was about the divide in the land—that is, if you consider the ocean and the meeting of the land as being a divide. And *The Fault Zone* was about another kind of fault in the landscape, and the freeways . . . I made a lot of photographs on intersections of major freeways, which is where all of those little communities—little at the time—began to take root and grow and to become the big communities that they are now. So that was my approach to LA, was to really look at all these different ways of dividing up the landscape through natural features and man-made features.

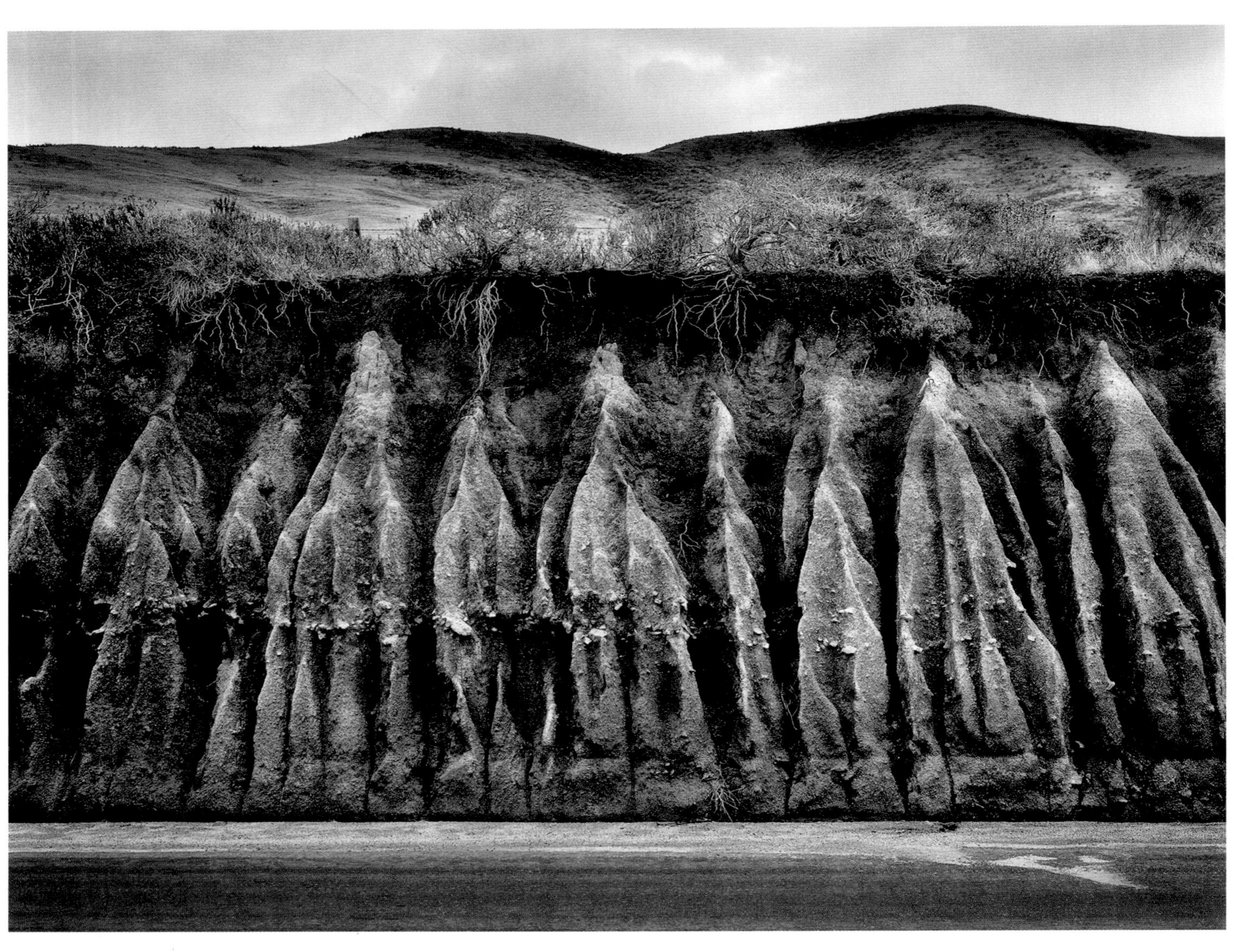

^ Plate 21 **Wynn Bullock**, Erosion, 1959, Center for Creative Photography: Wynn Bullock Archive

> Plate 22 **Brett Weston**, untitled, 1967, Los Angeles County Museum of Art

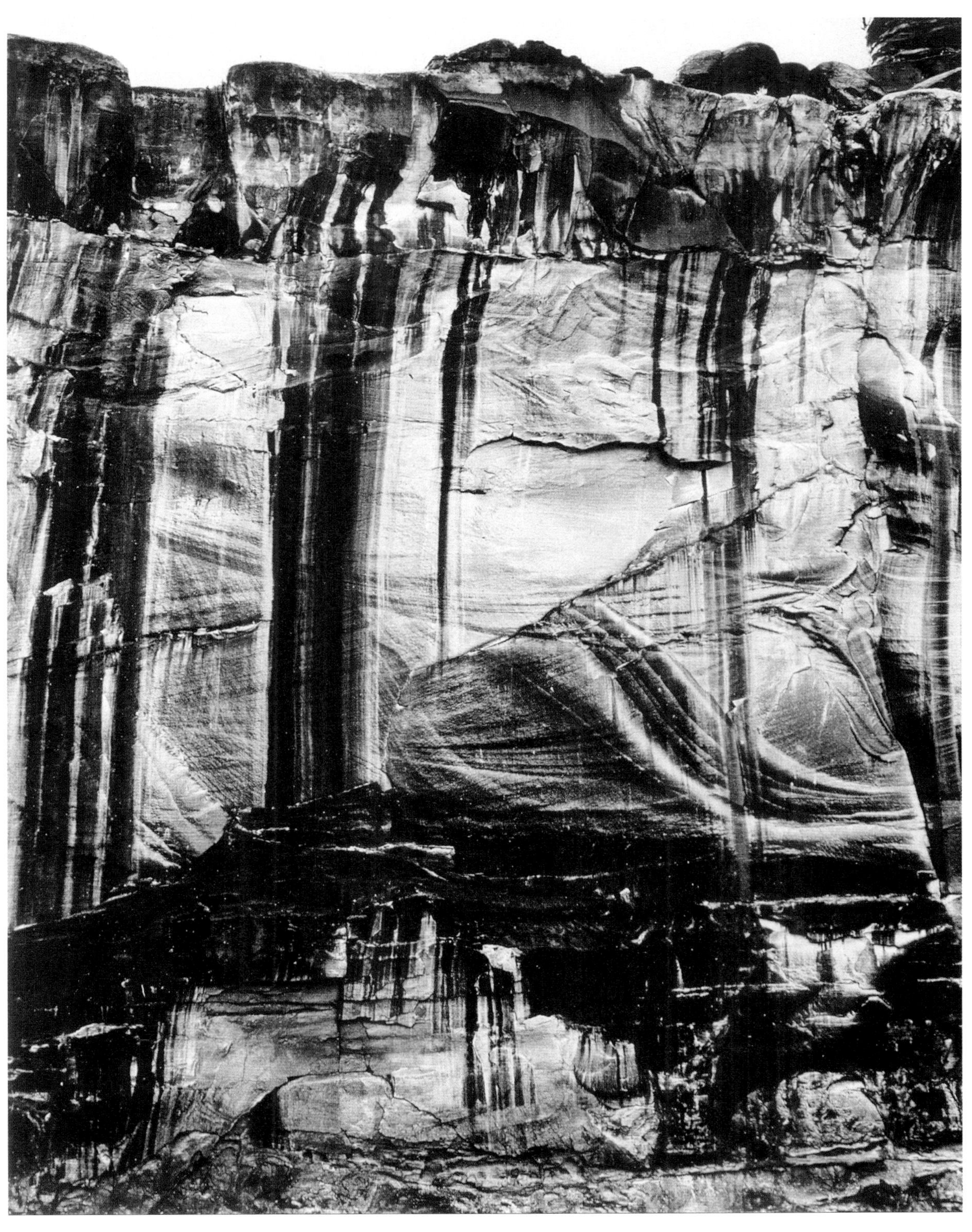

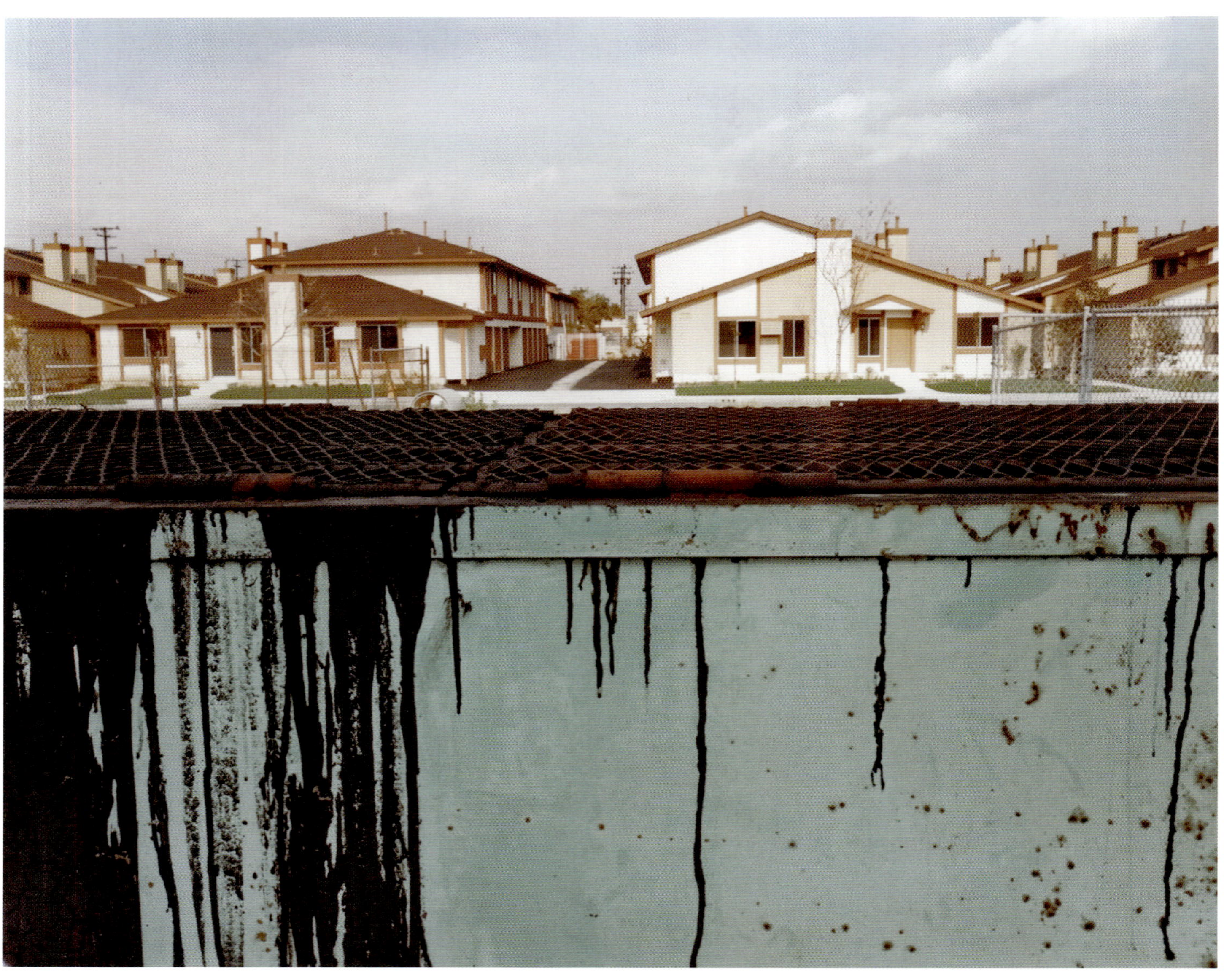

^ Plate 23 **Leland Rice**, Tar Covered Vat and Condominiums, Long Beach, California, 1980, chromogenic color print, courtesy of Leland Rice

> Plate 24 **Joel Sternfeld**, After a Flash Flood, Rancho Mirage, California, July 1979, chromogenic color print, Los Angeles County Museum of Art

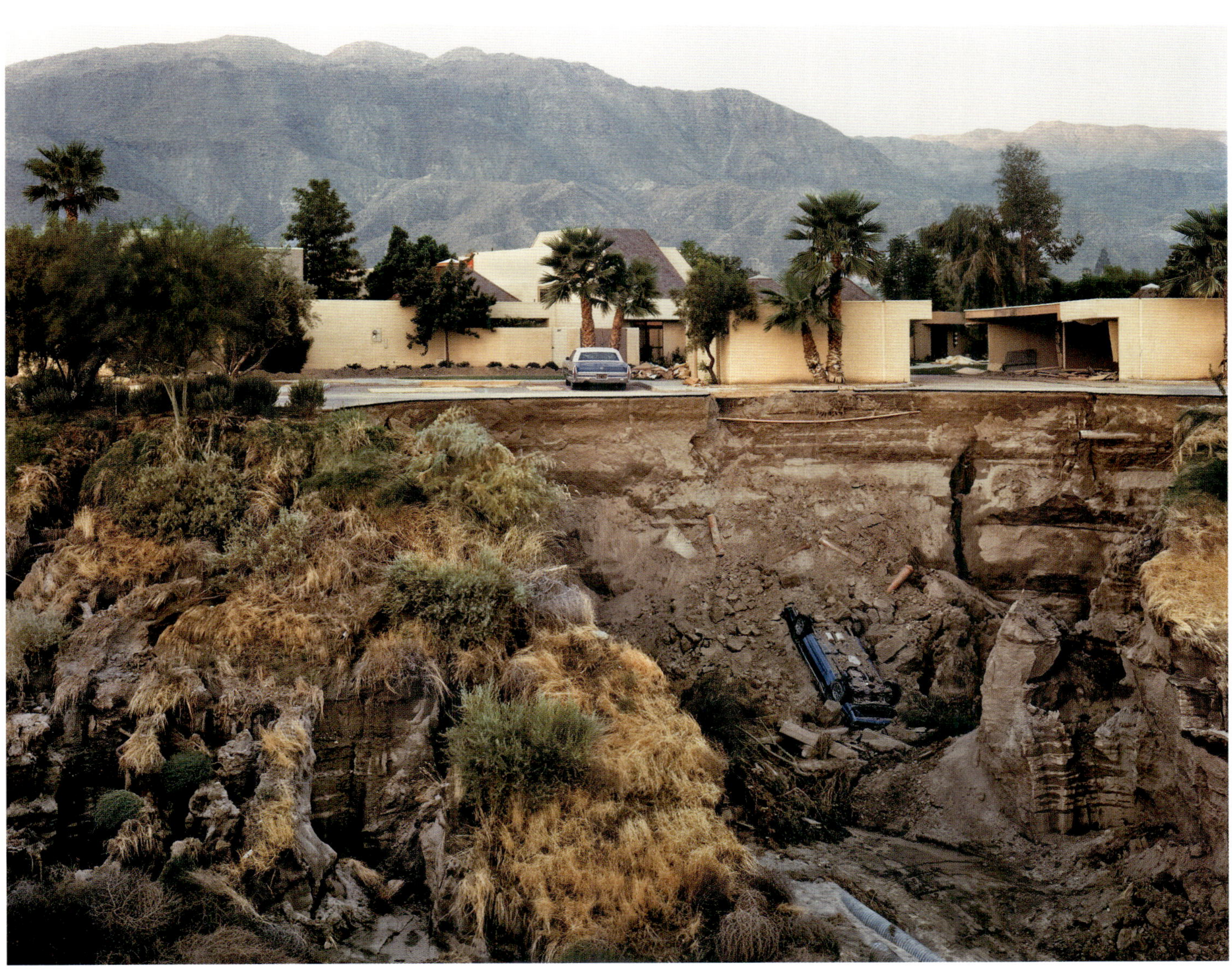

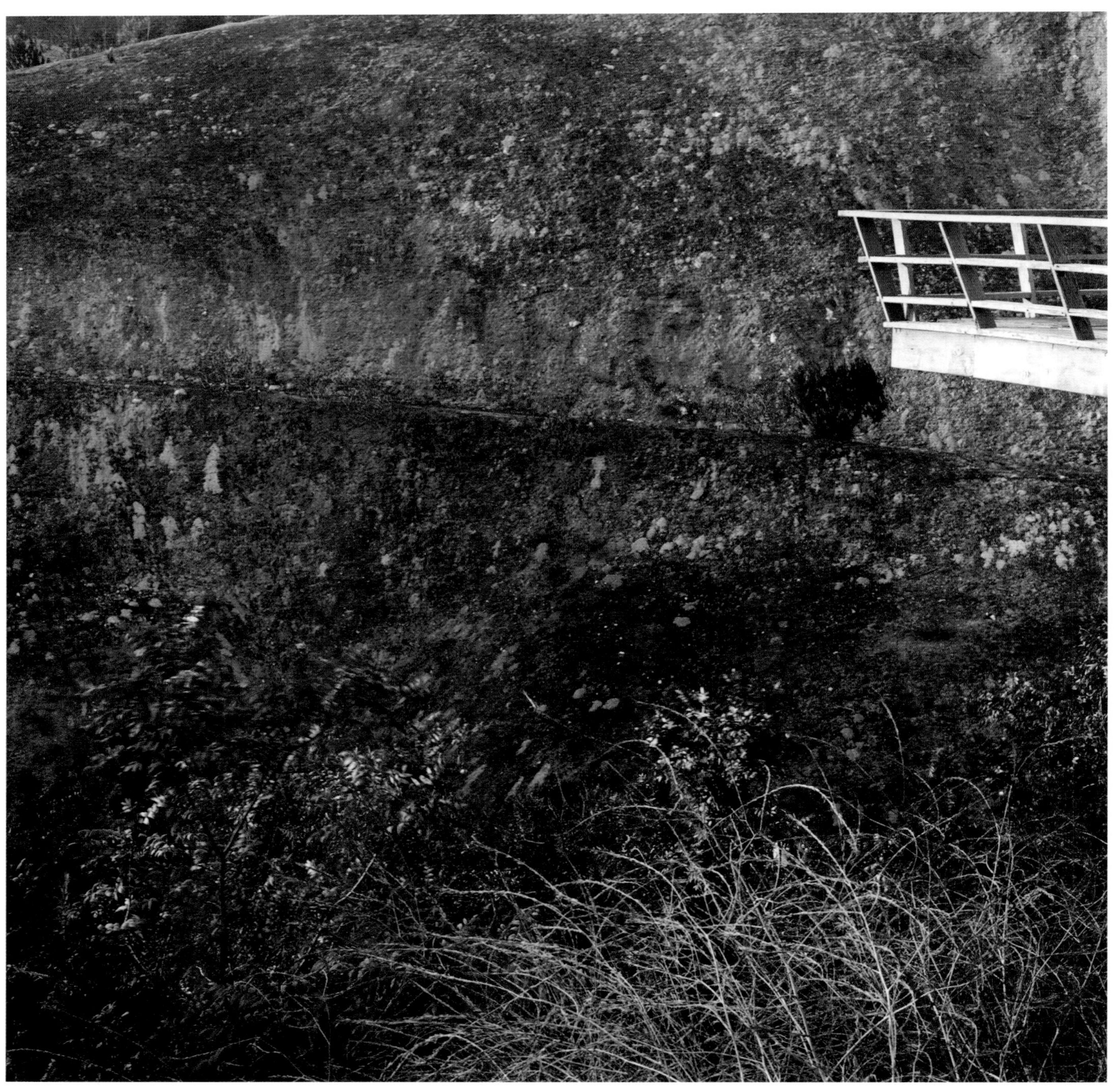

^ Plate 25 **Joe Deal,** Glendale, 1979, *The Fault Zone* portfolio, UCR/California Museum of Photography

> Plate 26 **Laurie Brown**, Land-Site Sketch #1, Irvine, California, 1978, courtesy of Laurie Brown

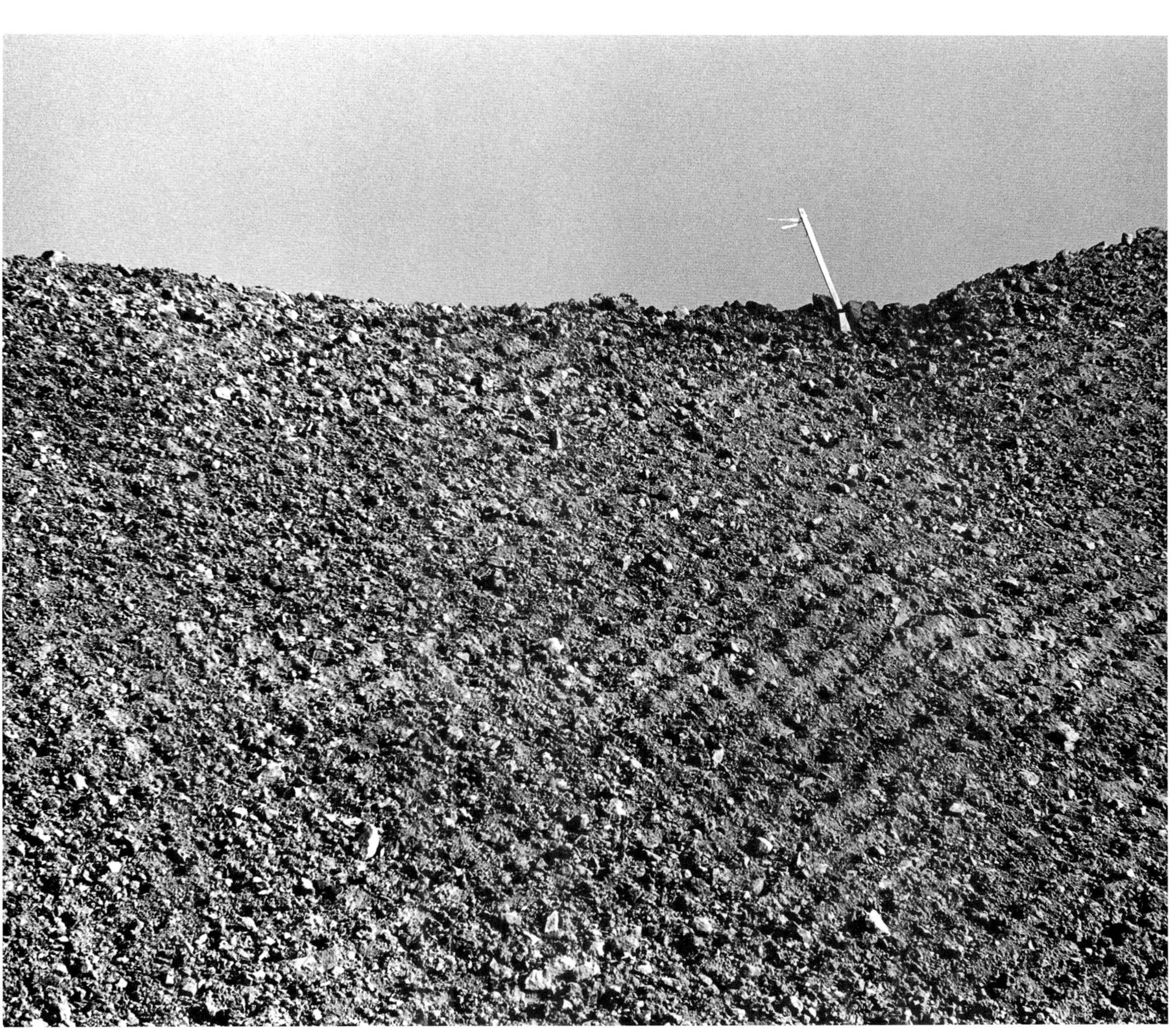

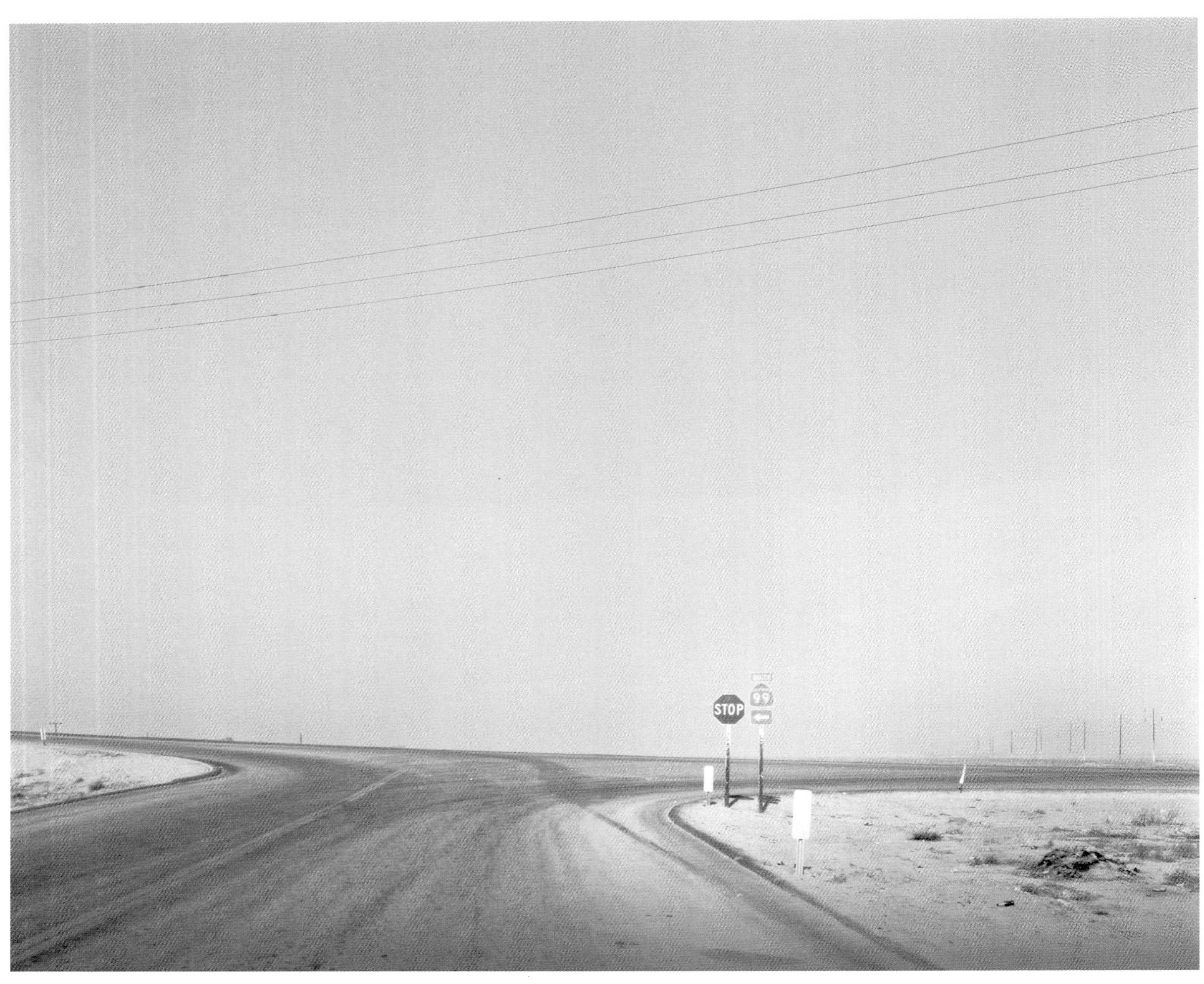

^ Plate 27 **Frank Gohlke**, Intersection, near Lebec, California, 1979 (printed 1981), Collection of David Knaus

> Plate 28 **Henry Wessel**, California, 1969, courtesy of Henry Wessel

STOP

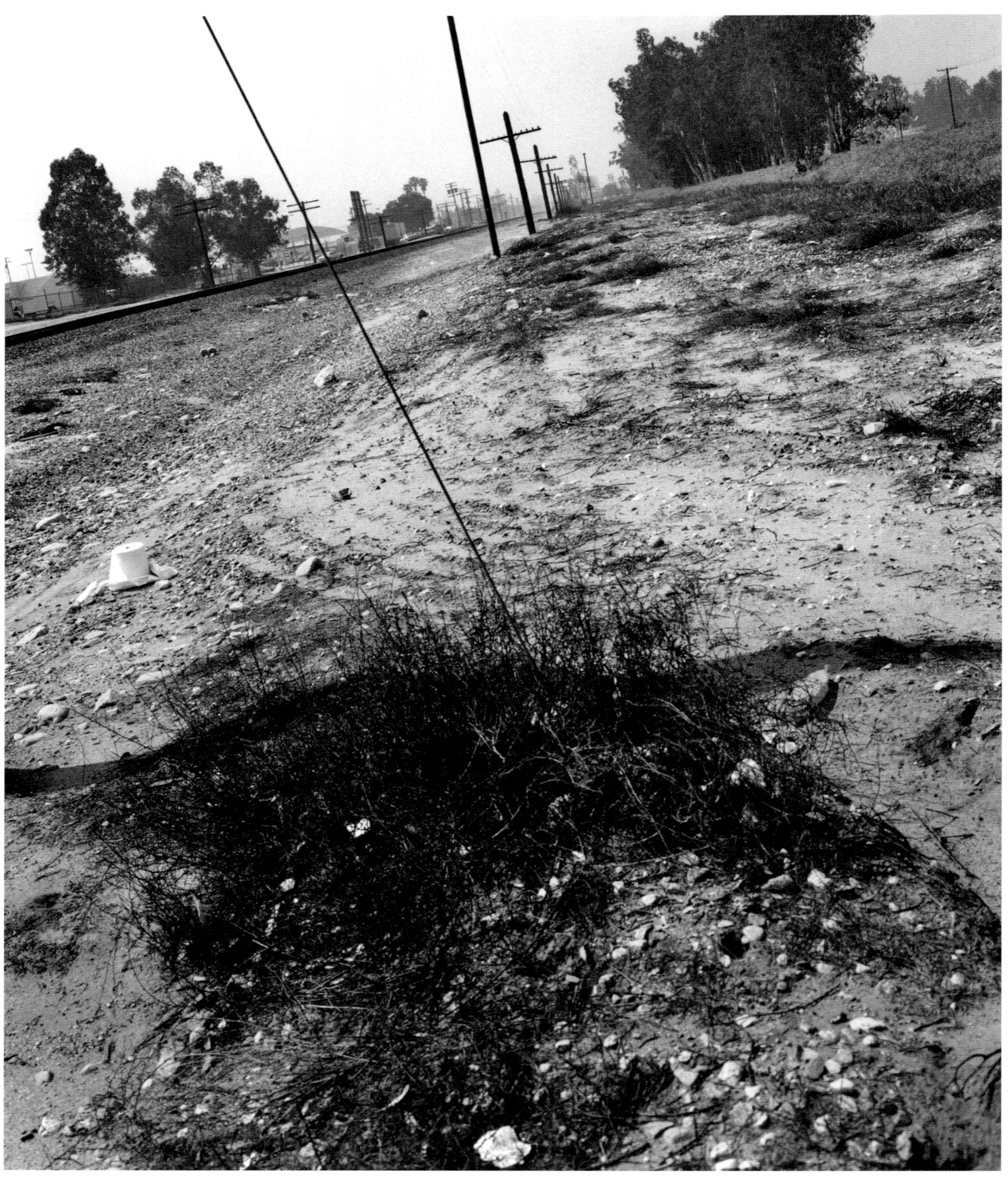

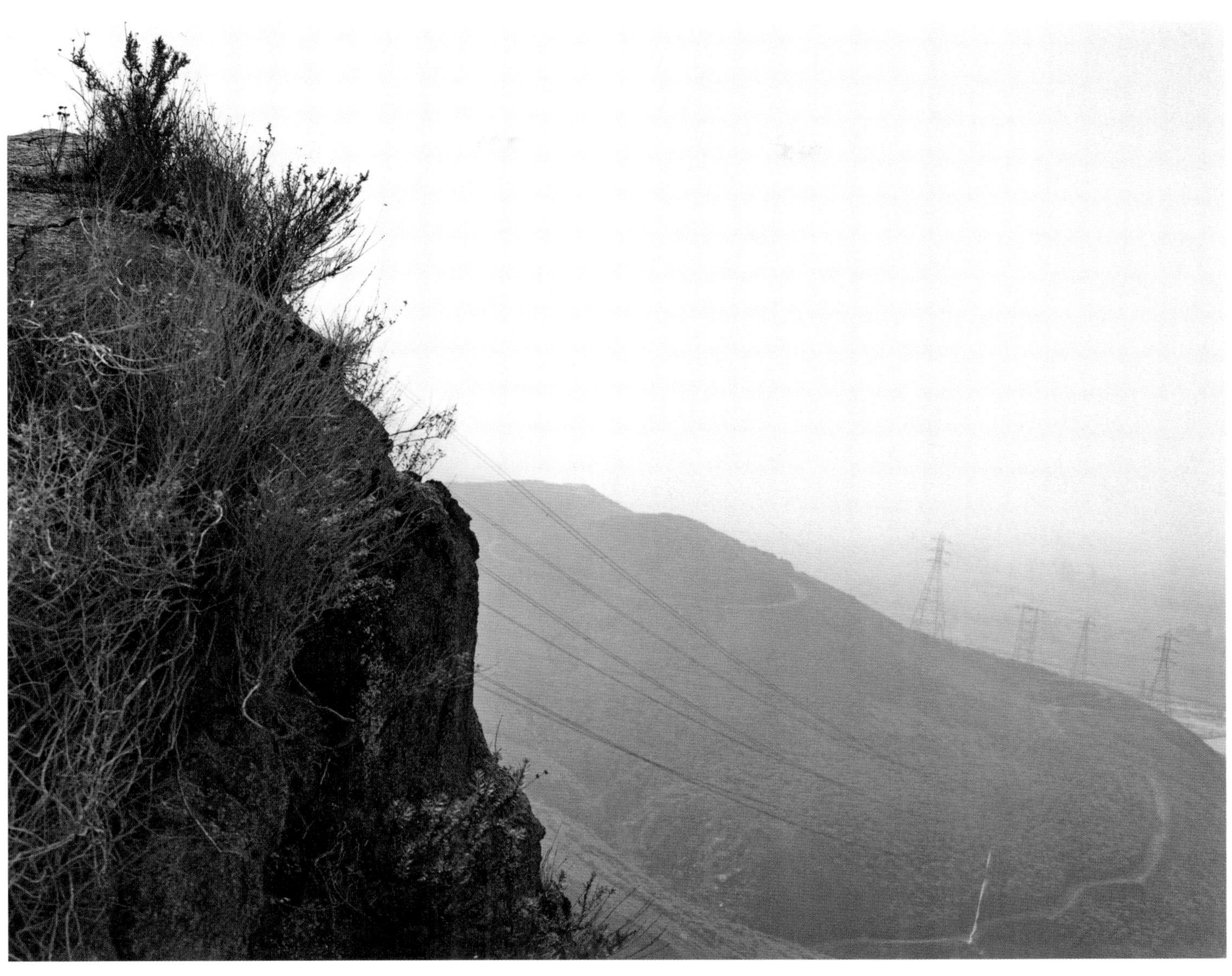

< Plate 29 **Robert Adams**, Ontario, California, 1983, Fraenkel Gallery

^ Plate 30 **Robert Adams**, La Loma Hills, Colton, California, 1983 (printed 1980s), Fraenkel Gallery

SUSAN LAXTON

"Nature" Photographed

The present epoch will perhaps be above all the epoch of space. We are in the epoch of simultaneity: we are in the epoch of juxtaposition, the epoch of the near and far, of the side-by-side, of the dispersed.

—Michel Foucault, *Of Other Spaces*

Looking back from the vantage point of the 21st century, girded by the comforts and discontents of the post-industrial global network, it is impossible not to identify Foucault's 1967 pronouncement of the spatial turn as prescient. Visual communication is now instant, rendering the dispersal of bodies and institutions unremarkable; and a general condition of deracination and displacement has guaranteed that juxtaposition, once a jarring visual strategy confined to avant-garde interventions, has become a cultural norm popularized by media practices ranging from alternative music to electronic dating.

This "spatial turn," identified at the very moment of California's "seismic shift" in photographic practices, places landscape photography in the foreground of representational strategies in the mid-to-late 20th century. Foucault's essay goes on to characterize the second half of the 20th century as a moment in which "our experience of the world is less that of a long life developing through time than that of a network that connects points and intersects with its own skein," a moment in which the "configuration," an assembly of relations (the series, the tree, or the grid) supersedes the rationality of historical narrative as the paradigmatic cultural structure of our moment.[1] Time is subordinated to space in this model, and space is conceived as an array of locations. "Our epoch," he concludes, "is one in which space takes for us the form of relations among sites."[2]

Viewed from within this context of the ascendancy of "the site," the radical shift in the aesthetics of California landscape photography that became visible in the 1970s with the exhibition *New Topographics: Photographs of a Man-Altered Landscape*, can be understood as a key development of a broader movement—one internationally felt and theoretically driven—a movement with the ambition to reach beyond the mere project of revising the conventions of "landscape" and "picturesque," to grasp *nature itself* as a cultural construction.[3] That is, within the context of the theoretical and political realignments of the second half of the 20th century, nature was put in scare quotes: it came to be understood as a concept with no currency prior to its formation as an idea, rather than a phenomenon that existed prior to its presumed opposite, culture.[4] Anxiety around this point would be substantial. It is not accidental that this same historical moment sees the rise of a cross-national, cross-disciplinary environmental movement and along with it, new areas of study: environmental psychology, geographical history, and landscape ecology—studies oriented away from the ethos of land use and focused instead on the ideological implications of an environment radically altered by the long dominance of industrial capitalism. At the same time that awareness of environmental degradation was seeping into consciousness, rendering the model of the "idealized view" untenable, the disappearance of nature before industry seemed to warrant the complete withdrawal of land use, encouraging the conversion of nature into to yet another circulating token in the system of exchange—a shift in material and practical terms that paralleled the one in philosophical discourse.[5]

Unprecedented views of the "man-altered landscape" produced by Joe Deal, Lewis Baltz, Robert Adams, and John Divola were avatars of this new awareness of "nature" reconceived as culture. This assertion seems much less extreme when one considers the way new perceptions of space were playing out in the site-spe-

Susan Laxton is an Assistant Professor specializing in the History of Photography in the Department of the History of Art at the University of California, Riverside.

cific art practices of the 1960s and 70s. Land art, for example, the work of Richard Long, Robert Smithson, Michael Heizer, and Mary Miss, explored a new set of critical possibilities made available through physical manipulations of the topography, and massive structures erected by Richard Serra, Robert Morris, and Alice Aycock intervened in the geographical configuration of space as extensively as did architecture.[6] Architecture itself gave early attention to the "symbolic landscape," as exemplified by Robert Venturi, Denise Scott-Brown, and Steven Izenour's *Learning from Las Vegas*, a project that began as a 1968 Yale studio and soon attained iconic status as a postmodern text.[7] Photography was implicated in most of these projects (Richard Long's site interventions, in their ephemerality, were particularly dependent on photography for dissemination and preservation), but it was to become integral to three prominent early assessments of site in conceptual art: Robert Smithson's *Monuments of Passaic* (1967), Dan Graham's *Homes for America* (1966–67), and Ed Ruscha's *Every Building on the Sunset Strip* (1966).

Smithson, Graham and Ruscha have been identified not as photographers but "artists using photography," figures whose combinatory works muddle the demarcations between categories and terms (is the art in the photograph, the text, the performance, or the concept?), just as poststructuralist theorists were intent on destabilizing the divide between nature and culture.[8] Smithson's ironic travelogue, *Monuments of Passaic,* appeared in *Artforum* illustrated with his own snapshots, identifying degraded industrial sites as the new pastoral. Dan Graham's *Homes for America* used photographs to condemn the anomic seriality of tract housing that was shaping suburban life, and like Smithson's "tour," his piece was designed to be published as a magazine layout rather than hung in a gallery, shifting the site of artistic dissemination out of the white cube and into the mailbox. The undistinguished images in Ruscha's fold-out book, *Every Building on the Sunset Strip,* used the plodding structure of the list to at once evoke the mechanicity, banality, and impersonality of the autoscape.[9] In all these cases, the photographs deployed were self-consciously amateurish, signaling a turn away from the conventions of beauty, expression, and fine printing and toward degradation and de-skilling as the sign of advanced art. And importantly, all these artists understood the work of art not as a singular image or object but as a configuration of elements (text, performance, photograph, and site of reproduction and distribution) that together produced the meaning of the piece.[10]

Considering photography's mythic alliance with nature, it would seem inevitable that the medium would be called on to represent the ideological implications of the built environment from the start. On the West Coast, Baltz's bleak images of Irvine Ranches date from 1967 and '68, and by 1971 John Divola had begun shooting deadpan typologies of the San Fernando Valley (fig. 1). But in Europe, landscape photography had already tipped into the postmodern as early as the late 1950s, when Bernd and Hilla Becher developed the photographic technique that was to become their hallmark. Their images of industrial architecture, and particularly the systematization with which they photographed them—always on axis, with the same even lighting, tonal range, scale, and point of view—seemed to mime the very conditions of production that had brought these buildings into existence, simultaneously exposing the conditions of seriality, repetition, and deracination that delimit photographic practices as well. Thus in frank opposition to the naturalized subjectivity of the photographer's "eye" dominant in European practices (Henri Cartier-Bresson's "decisive moment" comes to mind), the Bechers' recourse to a rigid system of production (made obvious by their insistence that the images always be hung as a group, in grid formation) foregrounded those aspects of the photograph that were constructed, rejecting its transparency along with its alignment with nature. And while photographs had long been presented sequentially, in albums and photographic books, it is here, in the artificiality of the gridded display, that we first see an insistence on reading photographs spatially, according to Foucault's terms: viewing them in multidirectional relation to one another, as opposed to temporally, as in the linear narrative of the book form, or singly, in affirmation of original vision. Seriality here works in resistance to both the list and the unique image: if Cartier-Bresson's "decisive moment" entailed freezing the most significant effects of nature into a single unified image, the Bechers' artificial and interchangeable pictures testify to the dawning distrust of this Romantic model. The gridded series presents a flexible array of options: an "indecisive moment."[11]

The spatial simultaneity of the Bechers' project is restated geographically in the social and physical structure of Los Angeles, making that city an ideal site for exploration of the visual qualities of the new spatial turn. The city's decentralized agglomeration of distinctive neighborhoods, commercial centers and ethnic and occupational groups are linked by a network of freeways that flatten it into a multidirectional lateral "unfolding," as opposed to a sequential hierarchy that could be experienced—or even described—in an orderly fashion.[12] One reads this plane of infinite extension differently in the work of Lewis Baltz and Joe Deal. Baltz's series of industrial parks in Irvine, made at a moment of pronounced industrial expansion in Orange County, subjects high modernist faith in geometric abstraction to the postmodern paradigm of infinite exchangeability. Viewed singly, the images justify the rectilinear severity of their architectural subjects

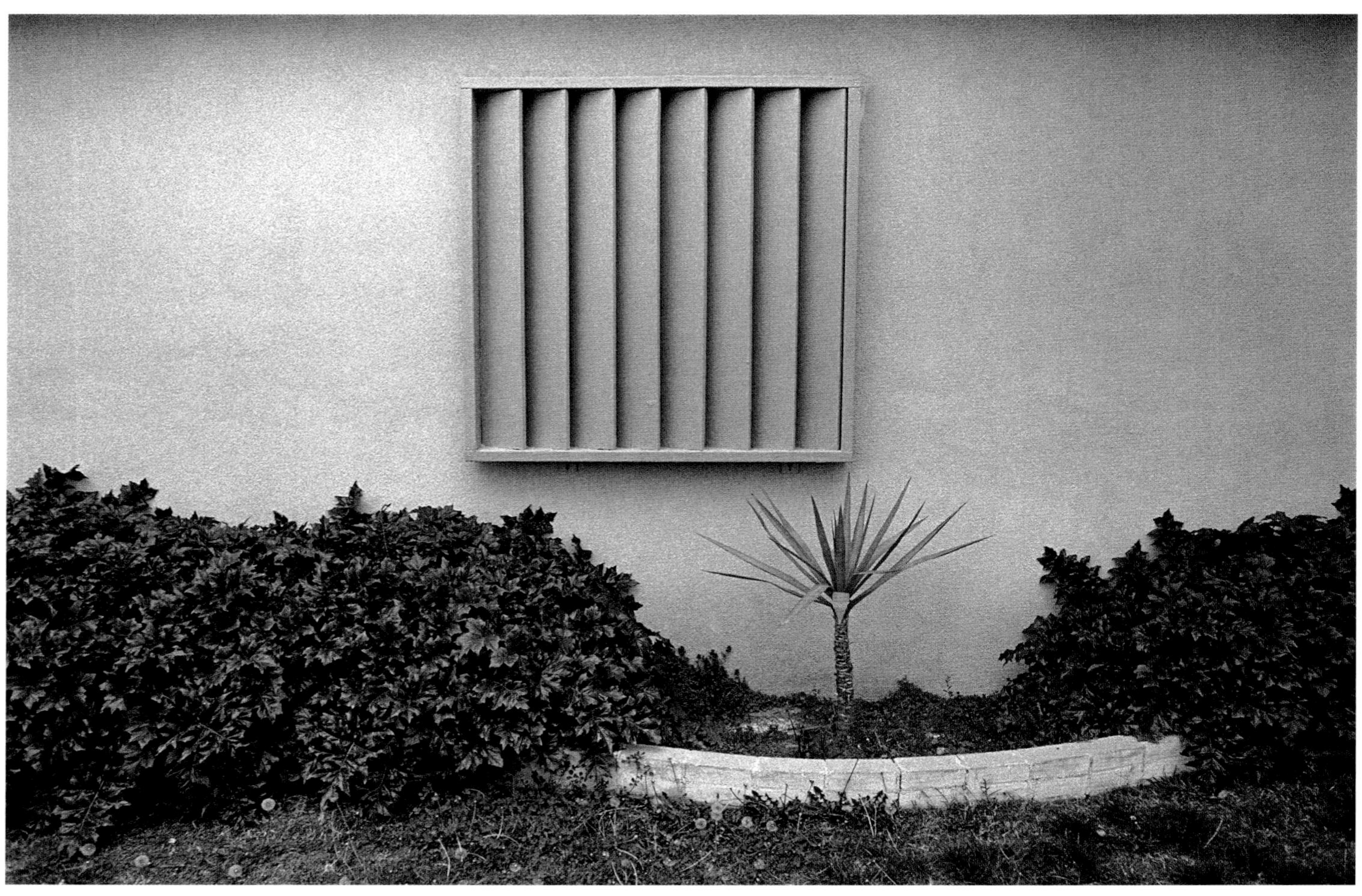

FIGURE 1. **John Divola**, untitled, *San Fernando Valley* series, 1971/73, courtesy of John Divola

with the photographic frame, to the point where "nature," in the form of the environmental context of the buildings, is pushed completely out of view. The harmoniously unified compositions that result are more a function of architectural forms flattened and fitted into the viewfinder than of the photographer's organizational vision. Grouped as a portfolio, the images take on the deadpan regularity of a typology, but one that is particularly airless and sterile, evoking a soul-deadening homogeneity across the group, and emphasizing the interchangeability of the structures and their indifference to their assigned functions. Baltz's oft-repeated remark, "Look at that . . . you don't know whether they're manufacturing pantyhose or megadeath," clearly indicates his alarm at the anonymity of the façades erected to mask the recently increased presence of the defense industry in the area.[13] But the statement also points to the spatial realities of the post-fordist industrial park itself: a gridded, regularized form, anomic, certainly, but as a function of the forced nonspecificity of the flexible space. Rethought this way, Baltz's "series" would hang admirably as a grid, where the eye's constant movement from one blank shell to the next would rehearse the fluid spatial structure of greater Los Angeles and of postmodern geographies at large—a movement without incident or development, and one that could generate seemingly infinite permutations.

These spatial coordinates map even more easily onto Joe Deal's topographies, in part because they depict the land with the same ruthless techniques of visual deracination as they do the buildings sited on it. If Deal's privileged, "omniscient" point of view, deployed systematically throughout this period, speaks of a patriarchal ownership of "nature" arrayed before the viewer, then certainly it is an ironic one. The high vantage point he adopts tilts the horizon up and out of the image, filling the frame to its edges with a flattened and nonhierarchical array of forms. A vertiginous disorientation displaces the proprietary stability of the fixed view from above, as the images abstract and disintegrate into ambiguous presentations. As unlocatable sites, these photographs become, effectively, any and all sites, and the infinite extension of the picture plane suggested by the high horizon line is thus reiterated at the level of the series as a whole: their structure pulls so far away from the pictorially framed conventions of landscape that the images could be abutted to configure a nearly continuously monotonous field. Deal's images, as well, respond to the diagrammatic structure of the grid, whose order is arbitrary and nonhierarchical, suggesting not the dynamism of dialectic but the open-ended register of simultaneous multiple readings, engendered by the sheer relation of one gridded nexus to another.

In his essay *On Other Spaces* Foucault claimed that we live in "heterogeneous space," space that is constituted by "a set of relations that delineate sites which are irreducible to one another and absolutely not superimposable on one another." The photographs of the artists under consideration here—those of Baltz and Deal, but also John Divola, whose exploration of chance and the constructed referent in his "Zuma" series destabilizes photographic transparency (pl. 35), and Robert Adams, whose exhausted landscapes reverse the terms of Romantic entropy—seem to have reduced these sites to interchangeable units, tokens that circulate and substitute with ease. This may be, in part, because these photographs tend toward the postmodern, cutting their images out of the continuum with full acknowledgment of the theoretical restructuring of photography. To this extent, photographic transparency can be compared to that of a mirror—at least in Foucault's imagining of it—for the mirror acts as a site of displacement, indicating the impossible situation of presence where presence cannot be.[14] Applied to photography, we can read here its utopian connotations—the illusion of the reflection of an idealized Nature (as represented in the work of Ansel Adams and Edward Weston)—but we could also locate in photography the same aspect of the mirror that caused Foucault to call it a "heterotopia": a site that counteracts reality simply by offering its mediated double, a double that forces the original site to reconfigure itself as a representation. In this case, that site is Nature, reflected back as "Nature."[15] Foucault's claim is that a heterotopia can function to order its space ideally, constructing an alternate reality to the chaos of lived reality (a compensatory heterotopia: Adams and Weston) or, it can create a "space of illusion that reveals real space, all the sites inside of which human life is partitioned, as even more illusory." The photographers of the "seismic shift" manage the latter. In doing so, they manifest the fluidity of space and site, which constitutes the way we live now, and that is a measure of their criticality.

Notes

1 Epigraph and this citation: Michel Foucault, Of Other Spaces, *Diacritics 16* (1) (Spring, 1986): 22–27. As noted by the editors of *Diacritics*, the essay was first published in 1984 as *Des Espaces Autres*, in the French journal *Architecture-Mouvement-Continuité*, but the text dates to 1967, as it is drawn from a lecture given by the author in March of that year.

2 Foucault (1986): 23.

3 *New Topographics: Photographs of a Man-Altered Landscape,* co-curated by William Jenkins and Joe Deal, was mounted at George Eastman House in Rochester, NY in 1975. The 1975 show has been reassessed in Britt Salvesen (ed.), *New Topographics: Robert Adams, Lewis Baltz, Bernd and Hilla Becher, Joe Deal, Frank Gohlke, Nicholas Nixon, John Schott, Stephen Shore, Henry Wessel, Jr.,* exh. cat. (Tucson, AZ: Center for Creative Photography, and Rochester, NY: George Eastman House, 2009).

4 See Bruce Brown and Noel Castree, *Remaking Reality: Nature at the Millennium* (London: Routledge, 1998).

5 Denis Cosgrove, *Social Formation and Symbolic Landscape* (Madison: University of Wisconsin Press, 1984, 1998): 231–32.

6 This postmodern expansion was first identified in Rosalind Krauss, Sculpture in the Expanded Field, *October 8* (Spring, 1979): 30–44.

7 Robert Venturi, Denise Scott Brown and Steven Izenour, *Learning from Las Vegas: The Forgotten Symbolism of Architectural Form,* revised edition (Cambridge, MA: MIT Press, 1977).

8 The case for "artists using photography" was first made by Jean Clair in his 1973 essay, *L'inconscient de la vue, Chroniques de l'art vivant 44* (November 1973): 6. It was compelling enough to have been carried forward in the form of nesting citations: Clair is referenced in Jean-Francois Chevrier's essay *Les aventures de la forme tableau dans l'histoire de la photographie*, in *Photo-Kunst: Arbeiten aus 150 Jahren*, exh. cat. (Stuttgart: Graphische Sammlung, Staatsgalerie Stuttgart, and Edition Cantz, 1989): 47–81. This title was, in turn, translated as Adventures of the Picture Form in the History of Photography, and included in Douglas Fogle, *The Last Picture Show: Artists Using Photography 1960–1982*, exh. cat. (Minneapolis: The Walker Art Center, 2003): 113–128.

9 "Autoscape" is the term Venturi, Scott-Brown and Izenour used to describe the Las Vegas strip, citing Ruscha's *Sunset Strip* as a source. *Learning from Las Vegas: The Forgotten Symbolism of Architectural Form*, revised edition (Cambridge, MA: MIT Press, 1977): 32.

10 For an historical account of the direct contact of the New Topographics photographers with these artists see Britt Salvesen (2009): 21–35.

11 It is significant that, in pulling together the 1975 *New Topographics* exhibition that introduced "Nature" photography, Jenkins and Deal included Bernd and Hilla Becher, linking their practice to that of the West Coast photographers' reassessments of photographic truth.

12 Edward Soja has called Los Angeles a "prototypos" of the post-fordist landscape. See Soja, *Postmodern Geographies: The Reassertion of Space in Critical Social Theory* (London: Verso, 1989): 2–3; 222.

13 The remark, made to curator Walter Hopps, is quoted in *Lewis Baltz: Rule Without Exception* (Albuquerque: University of New Mexico Press and Des Moines: Des Moines Art Center, 1990): 39; *cf* Salvesen (2009): 42. For a discussion of the growth of the aerospace and defense industry in Orange County in the 1960s, see Soja (1989): 190–291. Salvesen, in the section of her essay on Baltz's industrial park photographs, claims he had done a socioeconomic analysis before making the images. See Salvesen (2009): 42.

14 Foucault (1986): 24.

15 Foucault (1986): 24.

16 Foucault (1986): 27.

Lewis Baltz: *The Prototypes Works* were badly received by my classmates and professors at San Francisco Art Institute.

I was moving toward the point of view that the single photograph was not enough—insufficiently informational. Meanwhile John Coplans had mounted his *Serial Imagery* exhibition at the Pasadena Museum, identifying and analyzing the serial image from Monet to Warhol. I wanted to make a body of work in which the entire sequence, rather than the single image, was the unit. It was really then a question of finding a subject that could support such a project.

I was living in Monterey, a place where the classic photographers—the Westons, Wynn Bullock and Ansel Adams—came for a privileged view of nature. But my daily life very rarely took me to Point Lobos, or Yosemite; it took me to shopping centers, and gas stations and all the other unhealthy growth that flourished beside the highway. It was a landscape that no one else had much interest in looking at. Other than me. I was kind of interested in looking at it.

I had a fascination with sub-architecture, in a large degree because I came out of this environment. This is what I grew up with. The first walls I saw were cheap, fabricated stucco walls, you know, in my parents' house.

For me to address this environment was a kind of exorcism.

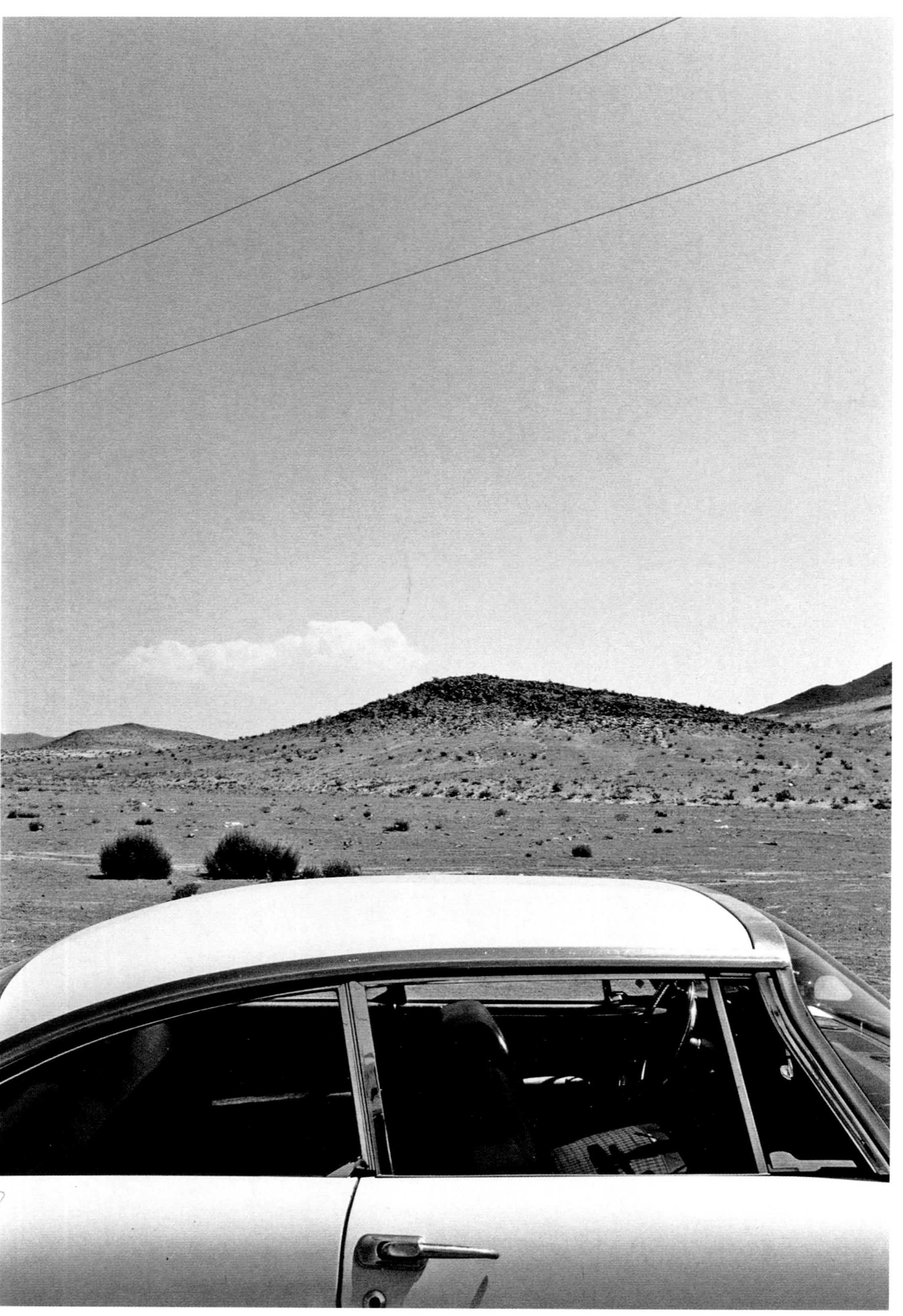

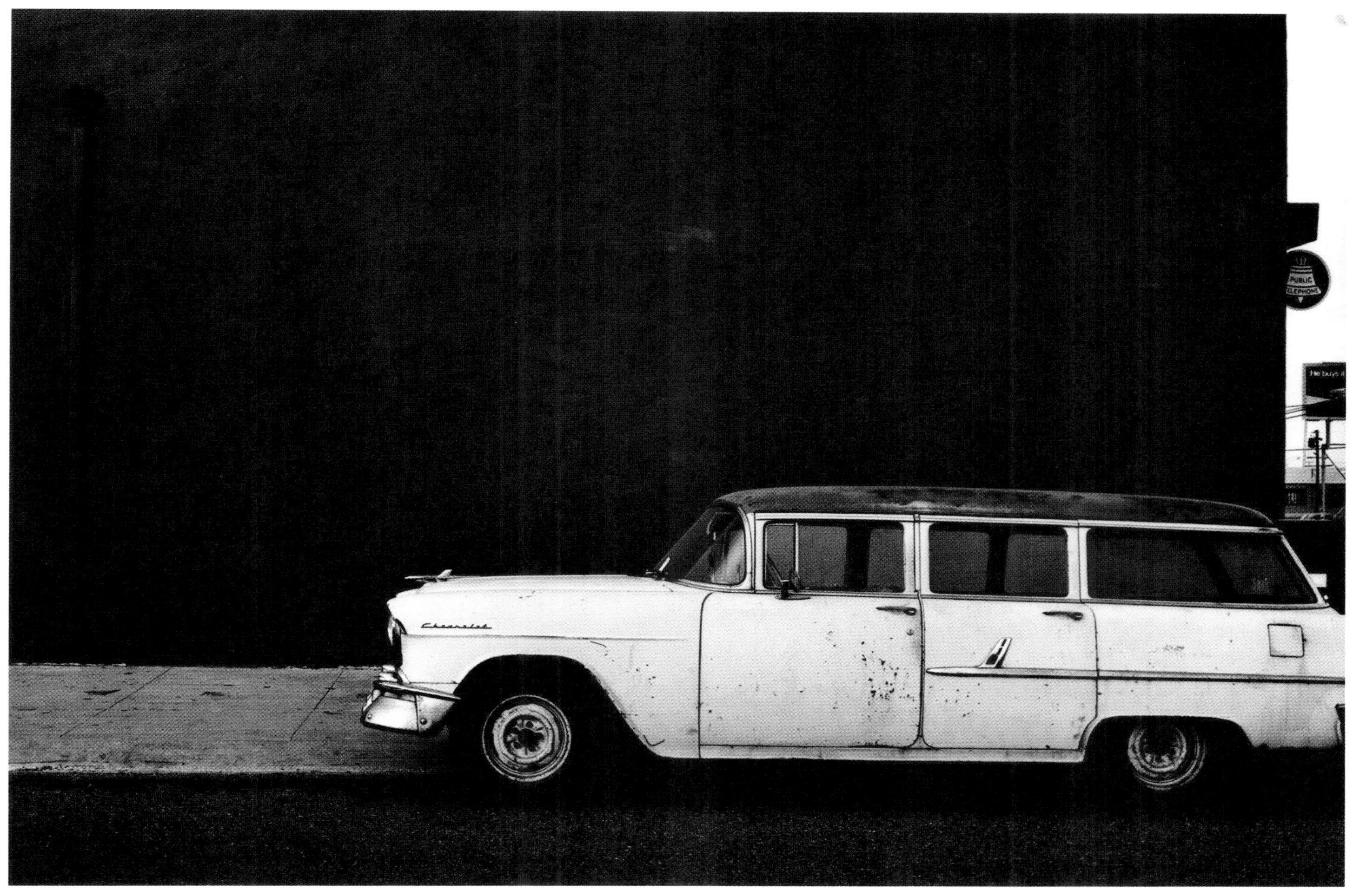

< Plate 31 **Victor Landweber**, untitled (Summer, California), 1969, Norton Simon Museum

^ Plate 32 **Lewis Baltz**, Santa Cruz, 1970, Los Angeles County Museum of Art

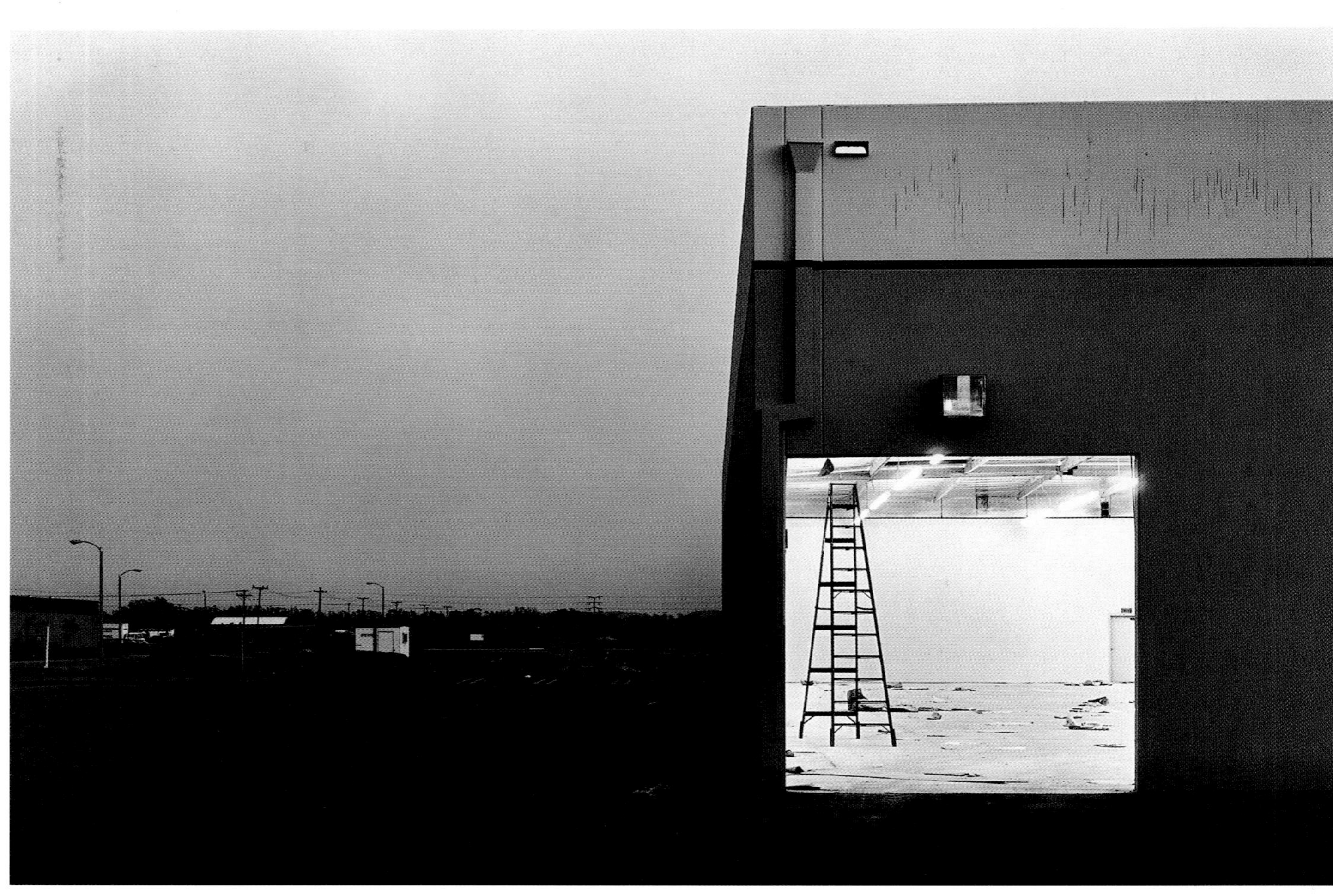

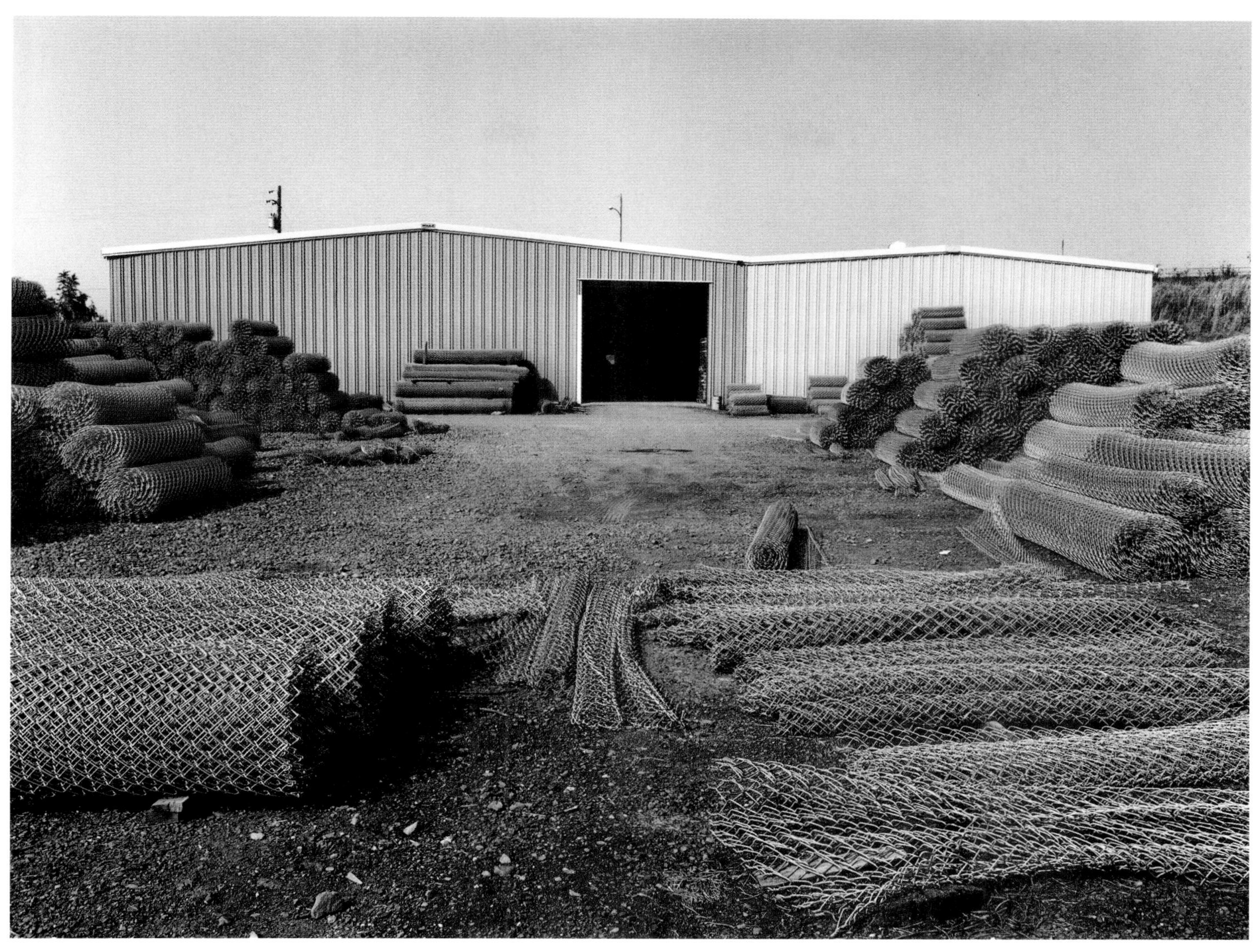

< Plate 33 **Lewis Baltz**, 26. West Wall, R-ohm Corporation, 16931 Milliken, Irvine, *New Industrial Parks near Irvine, California* series, 1974, Orange County Museum of Art

^ Plate 34 **Catherine Wagner**, untitled, 1978, *New California Views* portfolio, UCR/ California Museum of Photography

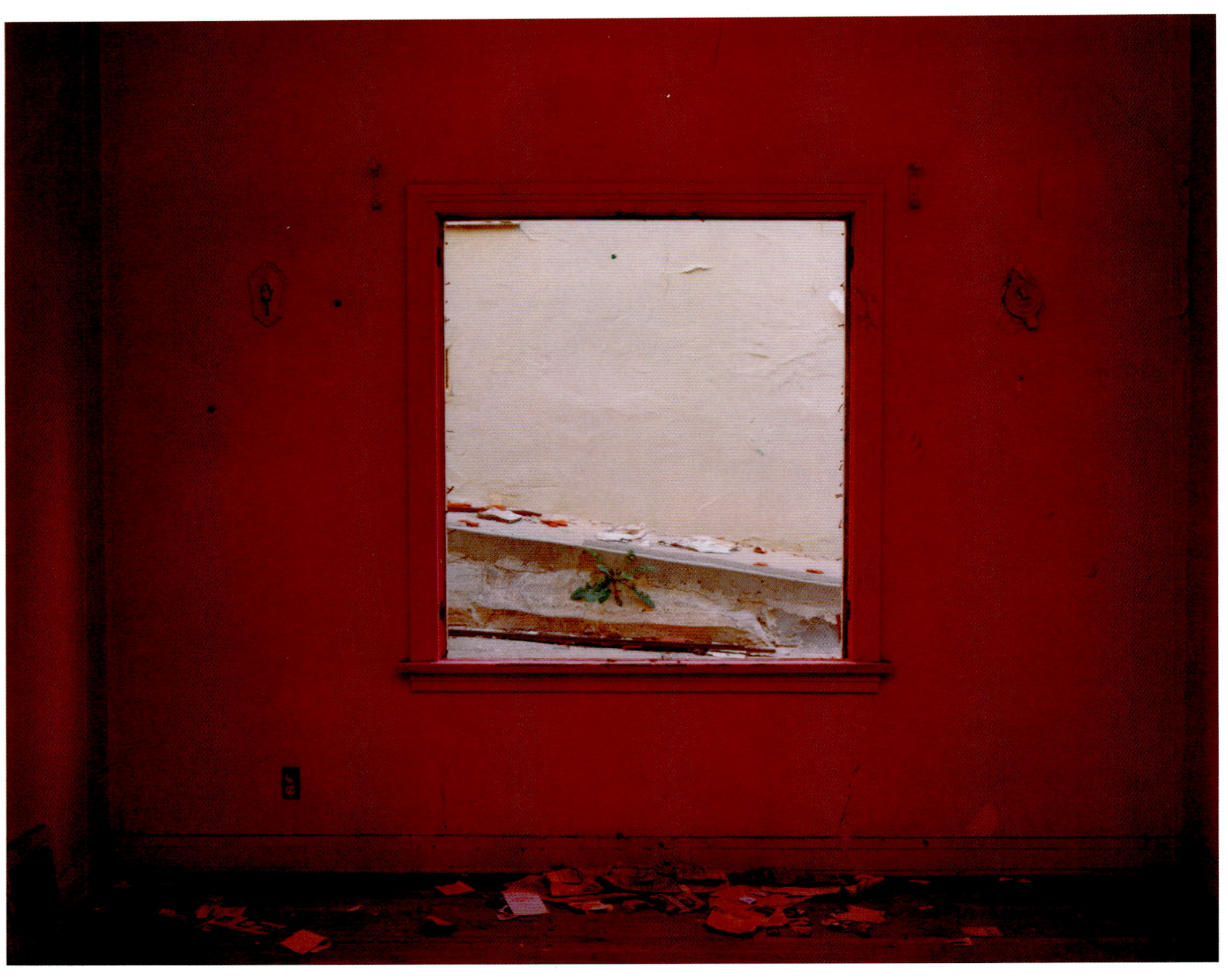

^ Plate 35 **John Divola**, untitled, 1978, *West Coast Now* portfolio, chromogenic color print, courtesy of John Divola

> Plate 36 **John Divola**, 75v2, *Vandalism* series, 1975 (printed 1993), courtesy of John Divola

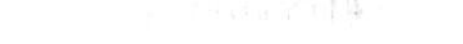

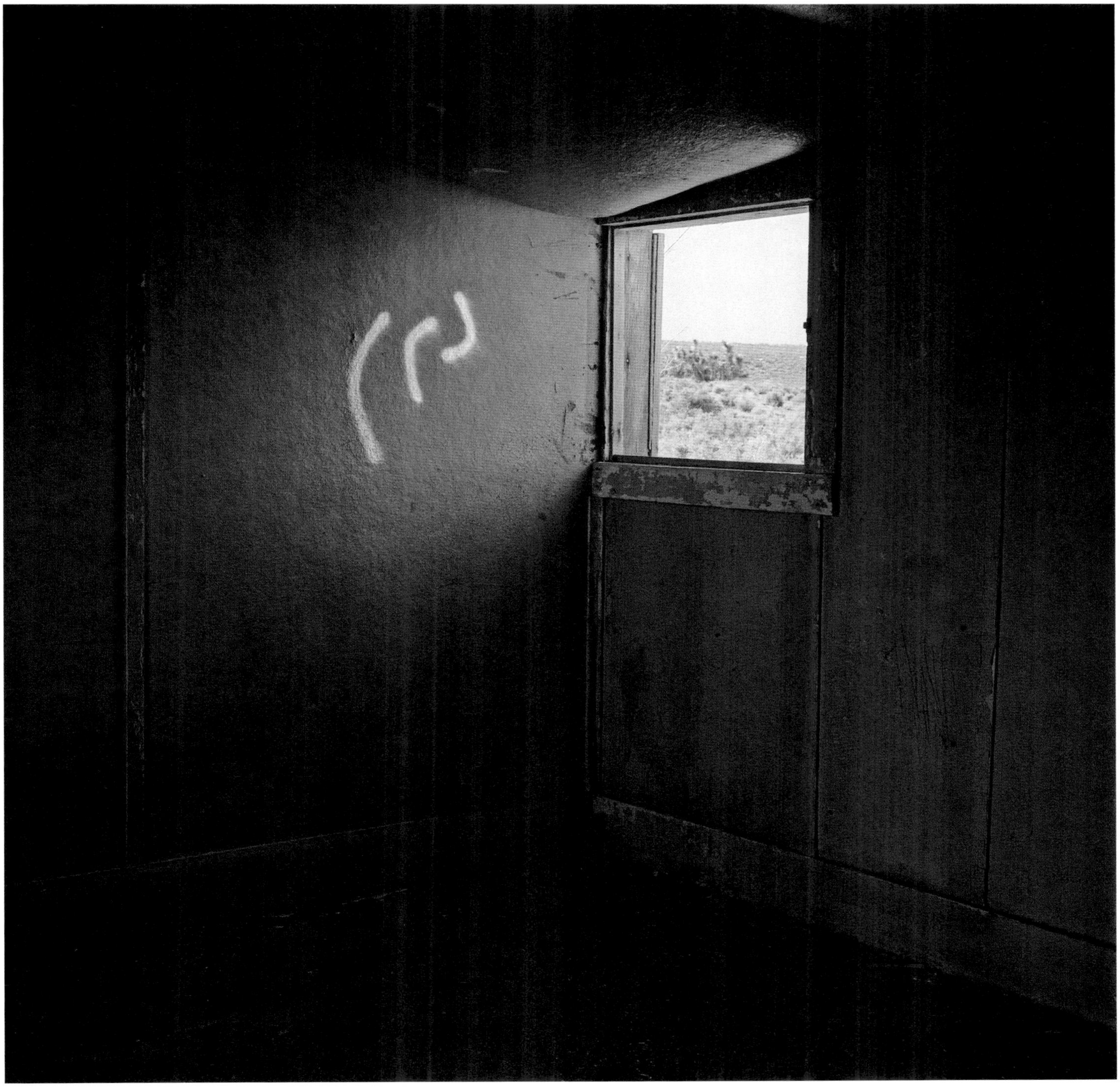

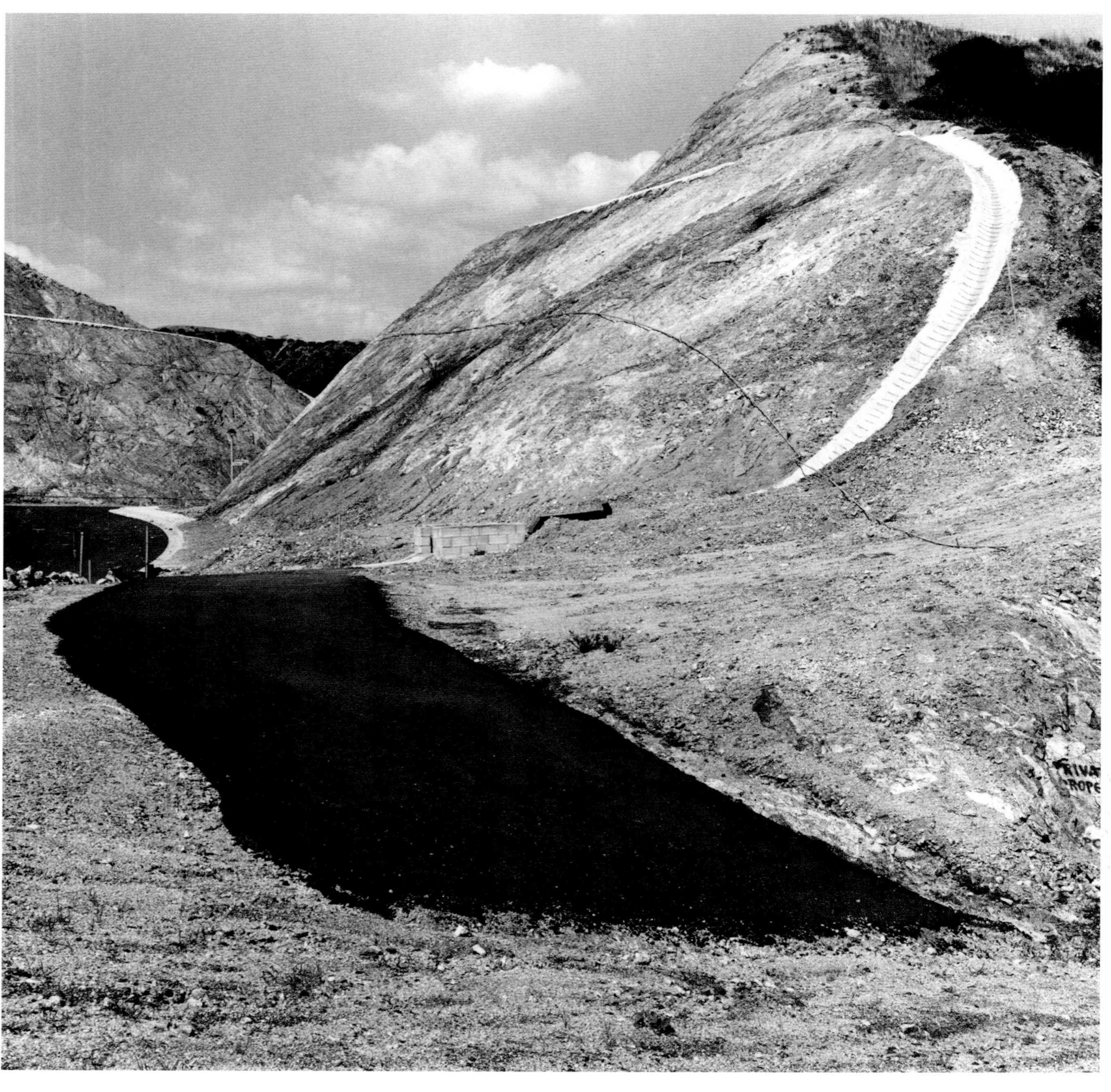

^ Plate 37 **Grant Rusk**, Glendale, 1980, courtesy of Grant Rusk

> Plate 38 **Phel Steinmetz**, Sunday, Palms to Pines Hwy, California, 1981, courtesy of Phel Steinmetz

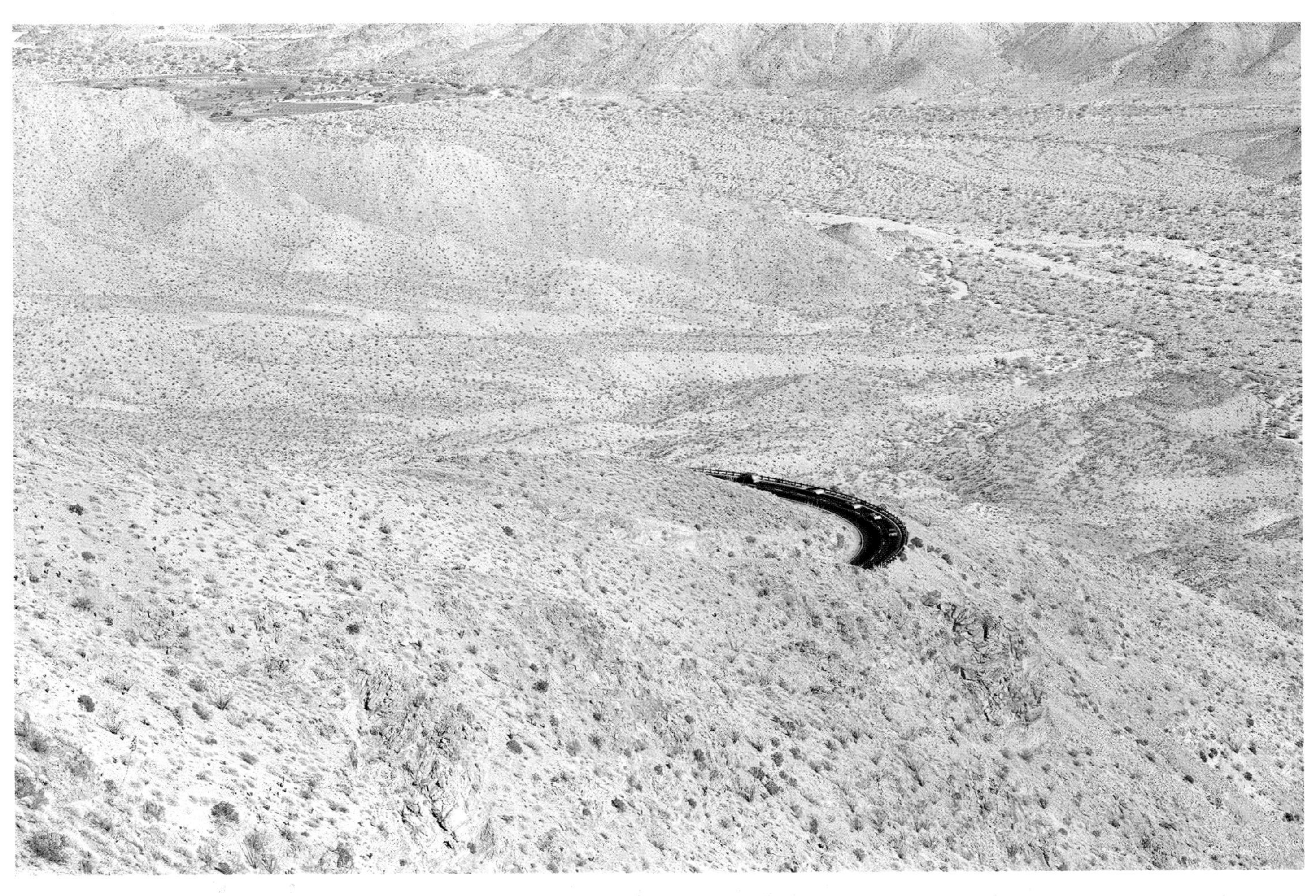

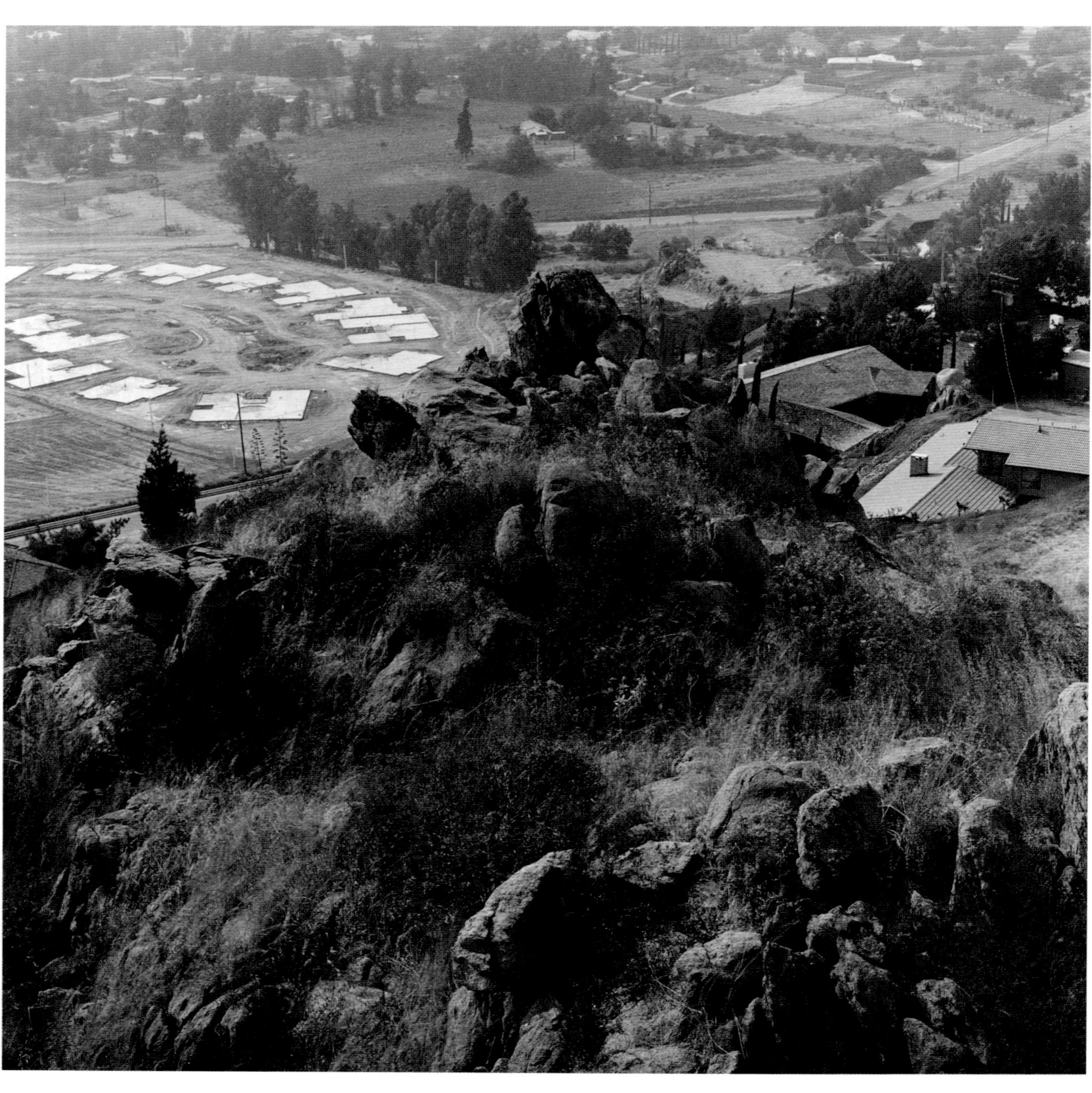

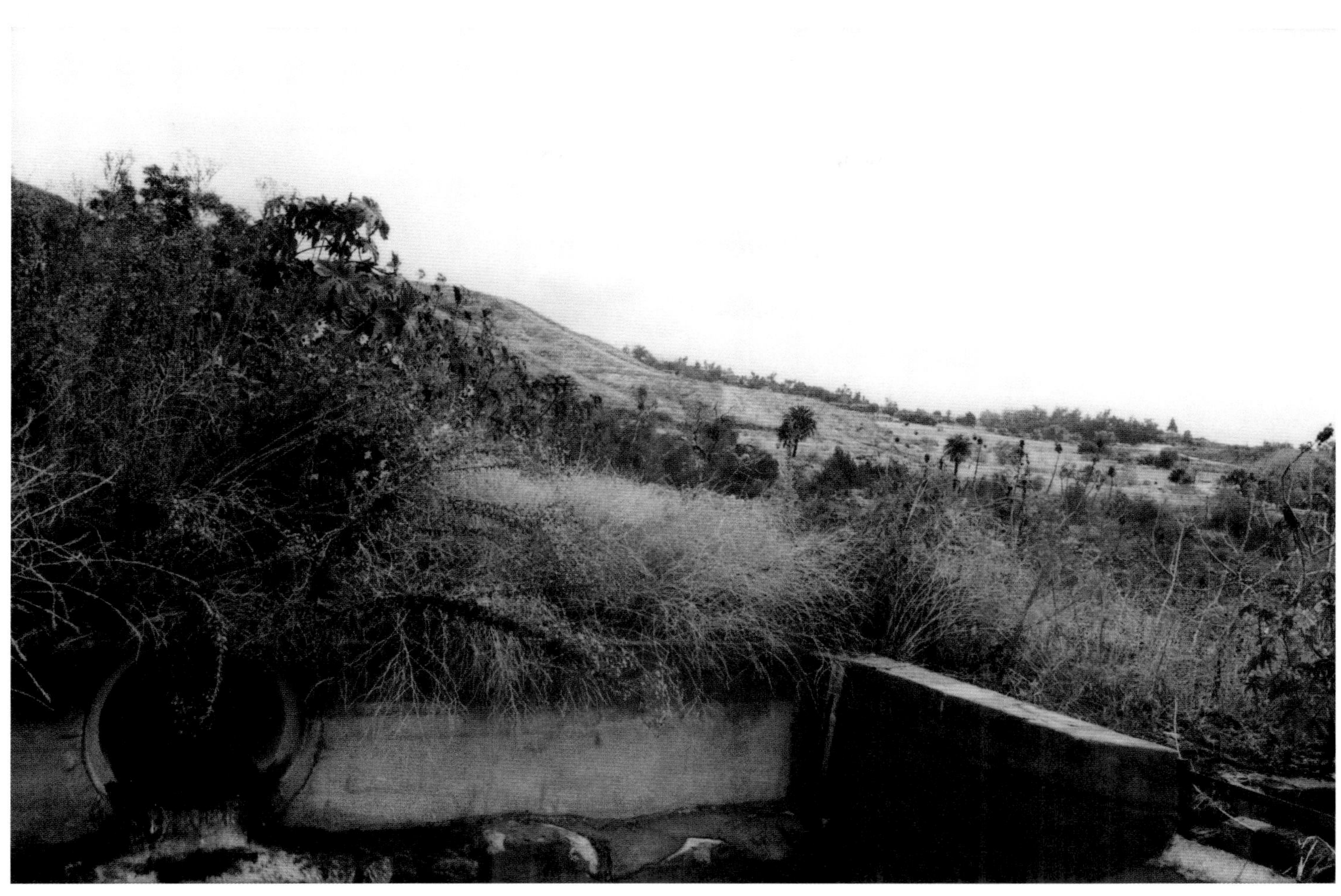

< Plate 39 **Joe Deal**, Colton, California, 1978, *The Fault Zone* portfolio, UCR/California Museum of Photography

^ Plate 40 **Sant Khalsa**, East Highland, California, 1982/83, *Intimate Landscapes* series, courtesy of Sant Khalsa

JASON WEEMS

The Meaning of Landscape in Late Twentieth-Century California Photography and Vice Versa

In 1953 the southern California photographer William Garnett produced a series of images depicting a walnut grove in the San Fernando Valley. Shot from the unstable perch of the photographer's Cessna monoplane, the images frame the landscape in a striking yet increasingly familiar aerial aspect. In one image, Garnett's vertical gaze—a straight-down line of sight that effaces the horizon and transforms landscape into surface—sheers the trees of their stature and trims their voluminous natural canopies into flattened snowflakes whose crystalline branch works sit with white-hot intensity on the surface of the image. Pressed into two dimensions by the conjoined gazes of airplane and camera, the trees no longer evoke illusions of organic fullness in either form or meaning. The natural dimensionality of the trees' living structure becomes an abstract pattern of marks that compresses the trees' canopies onto the same visual plane as the grass and vehicle tracks on the ground below. As is typical of aerial photography, the only visual indicator of the trees' stature derives from the tracery of their own empty shadows, which appear as spectral black lines upon the ground.

As depth gives way to surface and living environment surrenders to abstract spatiality, questions begin to emerge about the nature of the Garnett photograph and the displacement and reorientation it enacts. Garnett was perhaps first to recognize the image's flattening power and its implications. In a subsequent aerial photograph of the same landscape, the photographer captured a different vision of the grove wherein the trees had been bulldozed by real estate developers in preparation for the construction of tract homes. Showing the trees in a new and uprooted aspect, this second image enacts an eerie inversion of the original photograph. Pushed to the ground, the trees now fully reveal a more traditional arboreal profile. They become recognizable to the viewer *as if from ground level* only when they are splayed upon the earth like so many scientific specimens or, in another vein, lifeless corpses. In this second image the visual abstraction of Garnett's aerial viewpoint is counteracted, but at the cost of the landscape itself. What has been uprooted in Garnett's photograph is not only so many walnut trees, but also a way of looking at, relating to, and representing the phenomenal world.

Given the array of social, cultural, and artistic transformations sweeping California in the wake of World War II, the meaning of Garnett's two photographs can be sifted in many ways. Isolated in terms of formal artistic properties, the images demonstrate how machine technology and Modernist aesthetics might be combined to overturn naturalist illusion in favor of flatness and abstraction. Separated out as photographic documentation of real events and places, the images record as if in fact the changing situation of this particular stretch of California countryside at two specific points in time. Sieved for more metaphorical meanings, the changes thus recorded can be understood to offer commentaries both melancholic and strident on relationships between nature and culture, continuity and change, connection and alienation, and other dualities of modern experience. When mixed back together, these various components of the photograph—aesthetic, documentary, and metaphorical—can be said to constitute the complicated stew of characteristics, conceits, and conundrums that make photographs such beguilingly facile yet ultimately uncanny and impenetrable objects. Photographs are paradoxes; they are at once fact and fiction, reality and abstraction, continuous with time and space and attenuated

Jason Weems is an Assistant Professor specializing in the History of American Art in the Department of the History of Art at the University of California, Riverside.

from it, connected to one another by narrative but also irretrievably isolated in their singularity. As such Garnett's aerial photographs may operate most tellingly as ciphers of modernity, a condition which philosopher Marshall Berman (borrowing from Marx) has described as a "mode of vital experience" defined by fluidity, contradiction, and transformation: a world where "all that is solid melts into air."[1]

Berman's definition captures with rare elegance the complicated status of both California and photography in the postwar years. The state had long served as endpoint of American expansion—a place where 19th-century Manifest Destiny found its final horizon in the surf of the Pacific. After World War II, however, California emerged as a different kind of frontier whose potential was measured in terms not of physical space but rather of technological transformation. Already a staple provider of natural resources and agricultural products, during World War II the state, and especially Los Angeles, established itself as a seat of industrial output and technological development. As Patton's army trained for the North African landing on the arid plateaus of the Mojave, wartime industrialists filled southern California with shipyards, aircraft plants, and steel foundries. Scientists and engineers established research laboratories that focused on the development of wartime technology, from jet engines to plastic polymers. People streamed in from across the United States and the world to man these industries. Some to be sure were displaced Americans in the model of Steinbeck's Okies, but alongside them numbered trained specialists who brought not hard-luck stories, but advanced skills and a desire for social mobility. These ranks were further swelled by military enlistees for whom California was a jumping off point for the Pacific campaign and afterwards a permanent home base for the cultivation of middle-class lifestyles. The growing force of Hollywood in generating a new system of mass entertainment, which critic Theodore Adorno decried in 1944 as "the culture industry," further embellished southern California's status as a locus of modern America's tastes and desires.[2]

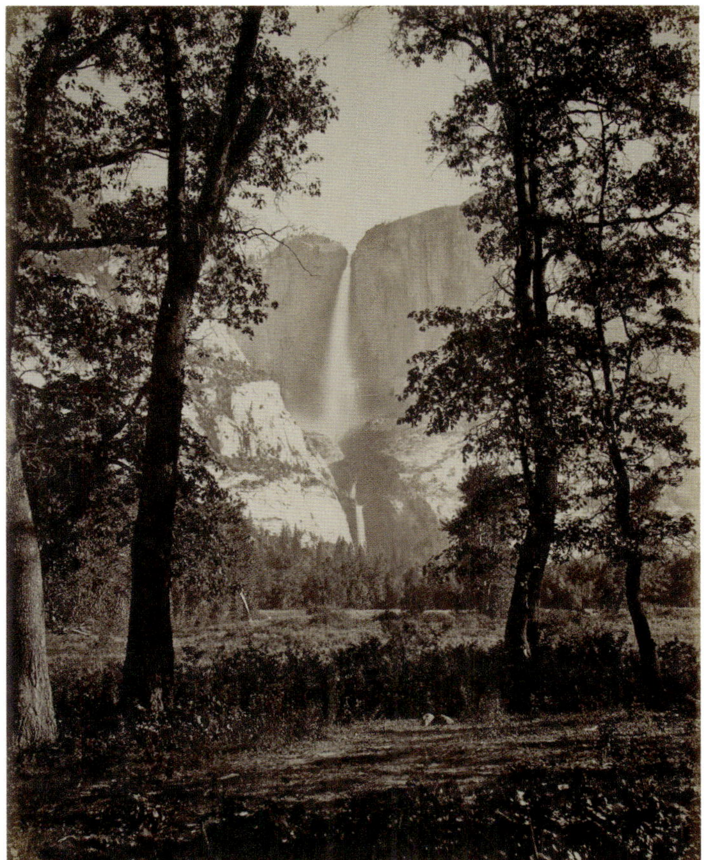

FIGURE 1. **Carleton Watkins**, The Falls, 2630 Feet, Yosemite Valley, 1866

The situation of California photography during these years proved equally fluid and unstable. Since the gold-driven booms of the mid-19th century, the camera had played an outsized and even commanding role in the shaping of the state's identity. Itinerant portrait makers offered the first views of California's mythic and mercurial promise in the guise of the eager prospectors that posed before their lenses. These studio practitioners soon were complemented by an august array of outdoor cameramen that included government survey photographers, artistic landscapists, and commercial view makers. Though diverse in training, practice, and purpose, by the beginning of the 20th century these photographers had cemented an iconography of California that put the landscape—predominantly natural, sometimes developed, but rarely compromised—squarely at its center.[3] Even today these images, from the geological survey photographs of Timothy O'Sullivan to the mammoth plates of Carleton Watkins and Eadweard Muybridge and the stereoscopic views and postcards of commercial outfits such as Keystone or the Detroit Photographic Company, continue to define an enduring (and increasingly overburdened) mythology of California as landscape (fig. 1).

Inevitably perhaps, this 19th-century photographic iconography of the California landscape as a never-diminishing wonder and resource began to fracture. As Peter Bacon Hales has suggested, the fragmentation was in part a result of the overwhelming success these early photographers achieved in their effort to distill a vast and diverse landscape into a limited repertoire of views.[4] Thus conventionalized and commodified, landscape photography in California and across much of the West came to bear an increasingly attenuated relationship to the specific physical and social circumstances of the places it pictured. Yet even as the medium's

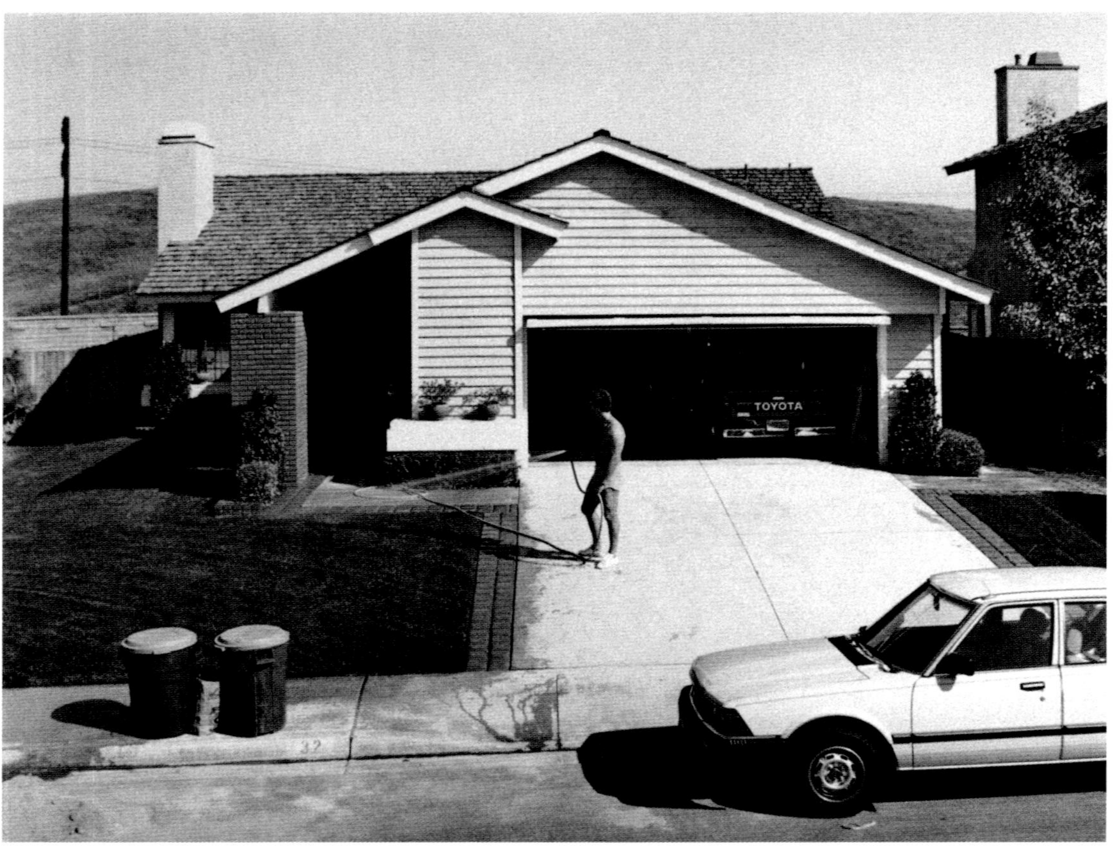

FIGURE 2. **Joe Deal**, *Watering, Phillips Ranch, California*, 1983, Collection of David Knaus

commercialist banality appeared to ossify, new outlooks onto the landscape emerged. By the 1930s especially, Sally Stein has argued, California photography "seemed poised to inaugurate the Depression with new modes of representation."[5] According to Stein, the changes took shape around two poles: the formalist and introspective nature studies of artist photographers like Ansel Adams and Edward Weston poised against the socially engaged documentary style championed by photographers like Dorothea Lange and codified by the New Deal. Divergent in many ways, the two trajectories coalesced in the demand that photographers give close attention to the specificity of California as location. For Lange, such focus entailed an unblinking (though not unmanipulated) scrutiny of the precarious sites and circumstances of Depression-era life, as captured in her well-known images of unemployed men and migrant families. By contrast, Adams's approach relied on the power of decontextualization to create images that isolated the landscape and encapsulated his vision of its aesthetic perfection. His 1944 photograph of Mount Williamson from the Japanese internment camp at Manzanar reveals something of his method as the quintessential particularity of the foreground boulders plays in complement to the transcendent light and ethereal haze of the mountain backdrop (pl. 1). That the photograph is staged from the infamous camp (which remains notably absent) speaks further to his sense of nature's cloistered monumentality.[6]

As this history suggests, California photography at the beginning of the postwar period was neither unified nor static. Yet if we compare Adams's Mount Williamson boulder field to a similar photograph taken by Lewis Baltz in 1983, some significant shifting does appear to have taken place (pl. 4). Adams framed his view in order to create a sense of isolated completeness that fixes both landscape and image (or landscape *as image*) into a condition of timeless self-sufficiency; Baltz's image disabuses its viewer of such possibilities. Pictured at a glancing downward angle and tightly framed to collapse illusionistic space into an unformed field of rubble, the photograph eviscerates the landscape of its scenic, iconic, and narrative components. Instead, Baltz transposed the landscape into an inescapably matter-of-fact specificity of time and space that invokes notions of an unmade and mundane, rather than an assured and transcendent, nature. Baltz's landscape is not a realm of epiphany, but a purposefully unremarkable and material site that is arrested by the camera into a condition of unremitting incompletion. This is not to suggest that Baltz meant his view to be static or empty.

Indeed, the varied size and jumbled layering of the gravel convey a sense of transient energy, while the tracks of earth-moving machines act as markers of industrial transformation. Nor is it to suggest, as some critics might, that the photograph is an anti-monument—an explicit and ironic negation of the landscape's iconicity.[7] Rather, Baltz's image conveys a notion of landscape experience wherein *stuff happens* (or not) out there, in decidedly non-emphatic but nonetheless interesting and meaningful ways.

The literature of postwar California art is saturated with an awareness of the shift toward the mundane and the material in landscape photography. Ironically, however, it often treats this turn to the everyday in all-too-emphatic terms. Following one line of thinking, the self-consciously banal images of Baltz, Ed Ruscha, Joe Deal, and others enacted an aggressive demystification of photography as a medium, from its oft ballyhooed claims of indexicality to its troublesome status as art. Often conjoined to this account is another trajectory wherein these same photographs serve up a withering critique of corporate, consumerist culture and its transformation of California into a land of crassness, superficiality and spectacle. In this interpretation, Deal's photographs of unevenly sodded backyards and suburban lawn watering (pl. 43, fig. 2) are said to reveal vapid middle-class desires and formulaic landscapes where, to borrow from a California-born Modernist from an earlier generation, "There is no there there."[8] Certainly such lines of thought recognize important questions that are embedded in the images and even more deeply, one might suspect, in the places they depict. Yet they also feed a narrative of postwar avant-gardism that posits the photographer in this instance, rather than the landscape, as self-contained and transcendent. Images may contact or be compromised by the world's banality, but the photographer remains somewhere else, above the fray.

One wonders what might happen if we shaped a model of postwar landscape photography wherein the argument for avant-gardism was not so clear cut—where the images of Garnett, Baltz, Deal, and the rest are perceived not as statements of conviction, but as open-ended markers of a more uncertain engagement with a landscape whose definition remained equally unfixed. Would we not see that, especially in the postwar years, the California landscape has served at best as an enigmatic icon of both nature and culture? As such, it embodies the fluidity and contradictions of West Coast culture on the whole. Its signature forms, from tract housing and superhighways to desert ruins and irrigated fields, evade simple explanation. The standard suburban development, after all, is simultaneously an architect's nightmare and family's dream. Is it not likely that these photographers' goals in focusing on the everyday landscape were not strident critique, but instead the development of an understanding, necessarily incomplete, of its possibilities? In this sense, their photographs are mundane in ways that are interesting, complicated, and ultimately, uncertain. This is the idea of modernity sketched by Berman, wherein forces of fluidity and transformation offer multiple, simultaneous, and even conflicting possibilities. This modernity happens, furthermore, in the most usual and nondescript of places.

Garnett, we know, did not like the landscape transformations captured in his photographs from the walnut grove. In 1958 he relocated from Los Angeles to Napa Valley to escape suburbanization, and in 1969 he provided the illustrations for Nathaniel Owings's *American Aesthetic*, a pivotal critique of postwar land-use practices.[9] In this sense, Garnett's work shares much in common with the transcendent impulses of Adams and Weston, or even Watkins and Muybridge. Yet he also finds unexpected potency and beauty in the supposed banality of postwar modernity, such as in his images of the Lakewood development in suburban Los Angeles. While such photographs can be viewed as transparent indictments of modern conformity, they also defy such simple analyses. Tract homes may not have the romantic appeal of walnut groves, but they are not without cultural—and even aesthetic—value.

Notes

1 Marshall Berman, *All That is Solid Melts into Air: The Experience of Modernity* (New York: Simon and Schuster, 1983): 15

2 Theodore Adorno and Max Horkheimer, The Culture Industry: Enlightenment as Mass Deception, in *The Dialectic of Enlightenment* (New York: Herder and Herder, 1972): 120–167. Adorno and Horkheimer completed the text while residing in Los Angeles. The city and its entertainment industry have been widely interpreted as having a formative influence on their critique.

3 The bibliography on 19th-century photography in California and the West is both broad and deep. For a compelling overview of the medium's role in our understanding of the western landscape, see Peter Bacon Hales, American Views and the Romance of Modernization, in Martha A. Sandweiss, ed. *Photography in Nineteenth-Century America* (Fort Worth, TX: The Amon Carter Museum; and New York: Harry N. Abrams, 1991): 205–257.

4 Hales (1991): 241 and *passim*.

5 Sally Stein, On Location: The Placement (and Replacement) of California in 1930s Photography, in Stephanie Baron, ed. *Reading California: Art, Image and Identity, 1900–2000* (Berkeley: University of California Press, 2000): 173

6 Adams devoted substantial efforts to documenting the Manzanar camp at the end of World War II and was highly critical of the internment both during and after the war. See Ansel Adams, *Born Free and Equal: The Story of Loyal Japanese Americans* (New York: U.S. Camera, 1944)

7 My understanding of the anti-monument in relation to the American West comes out of the literature on 1960s earth art. For example, see Suzanne Boettger, *Earthworks: Art and Landscape in the Sixties* (Berkeley: University of California Press, 2004): 244 and *passim*.

8 Gertrude Stein, *Everybody's Autobiography* (New York, Random House, 1937).

9 Nathaniel Owings, *The American Aesthetic*. Photographs by William Garnett (New York, Harper and Row, 1969).

Lewis Baltz: You should recall that in the ’60s the dominant theoretical position was a glorification of subjectivity and the “otherness” of the depicted subject, an absurd extension of Stieglitz’s theory of equivalents.

This set of notions took as its goal the mystification of the phenomenal world and the creation of an emotional parallel universe where the photographic subject became merely a vehicle for the photographers’ emotions. This very dubious idea was made even more questionable by its elevation of a hierarchy of emotive subjects: reflections in tidepools, weathered wood, dead birds, and such like. Subjects such as these served as free-floating “equivalents” for the generation of photographers preceding my own. Naturally, my generation wanted no part of this obsolete thinking. We sought its opposite, an objectivity so pure that the artist vanished.

This is mostly interesting as polemic. In fact it’s impossible to make a wholly subjective image, and it is also impossible to make an image that is purely objective. But there are significant differences, and if you plotted a spectrum, I was way over on the objective side. Which by no means made my work apolitical. But it was my conviction that if one wished to critique an institution, a practice, or an ideology, the most effective way to do so was to dispassionately assemble a case against it, rather like a legal brief.

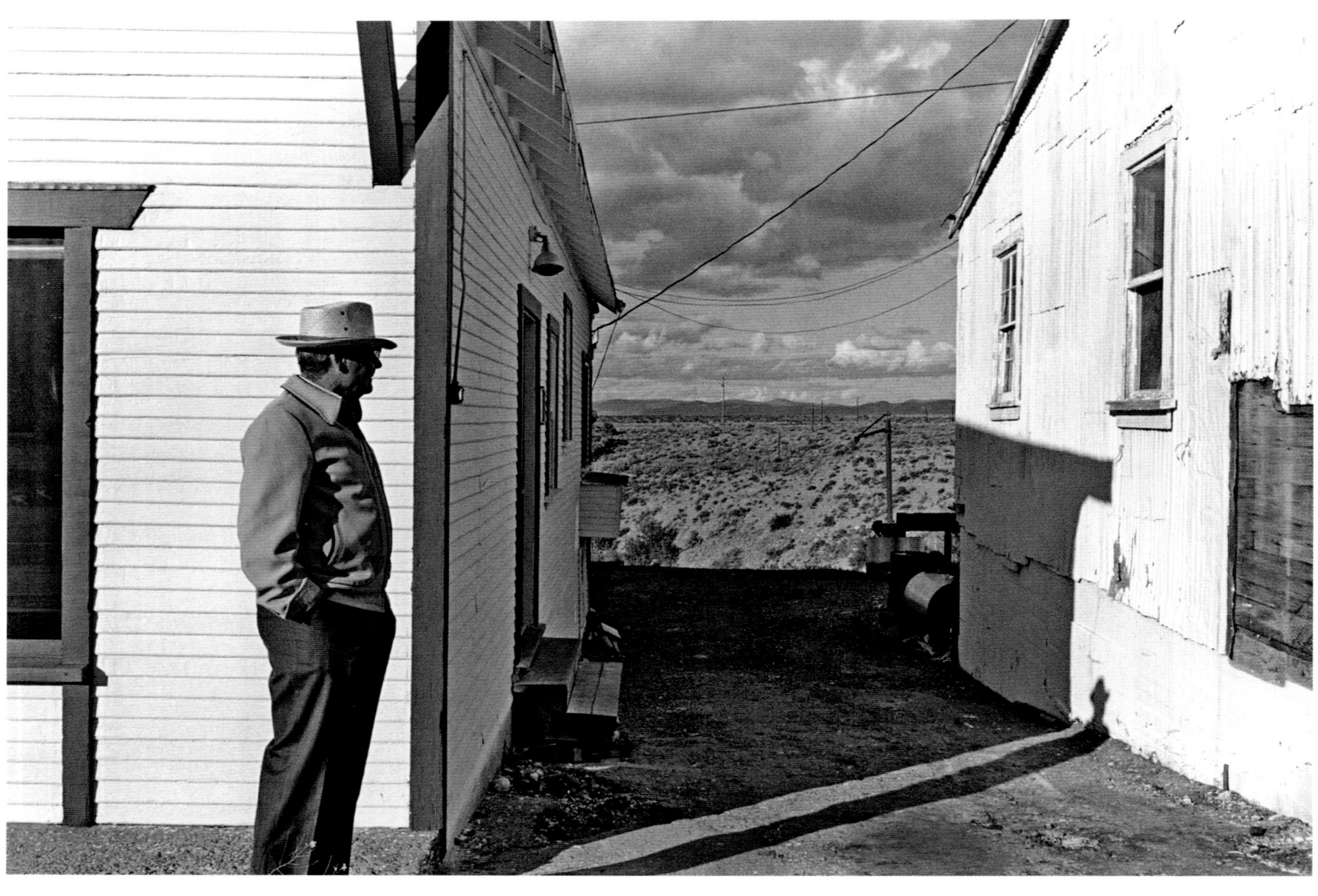

^ Plate 41 **Henry Wessel**, Nevada, 1975, Collection of David Knaus

> Plate 42 **Michael J. Elderman**, The World's Playground—Steel Pier, 1983, *Sideviews* portfolio, UCR/California Museum of Photography

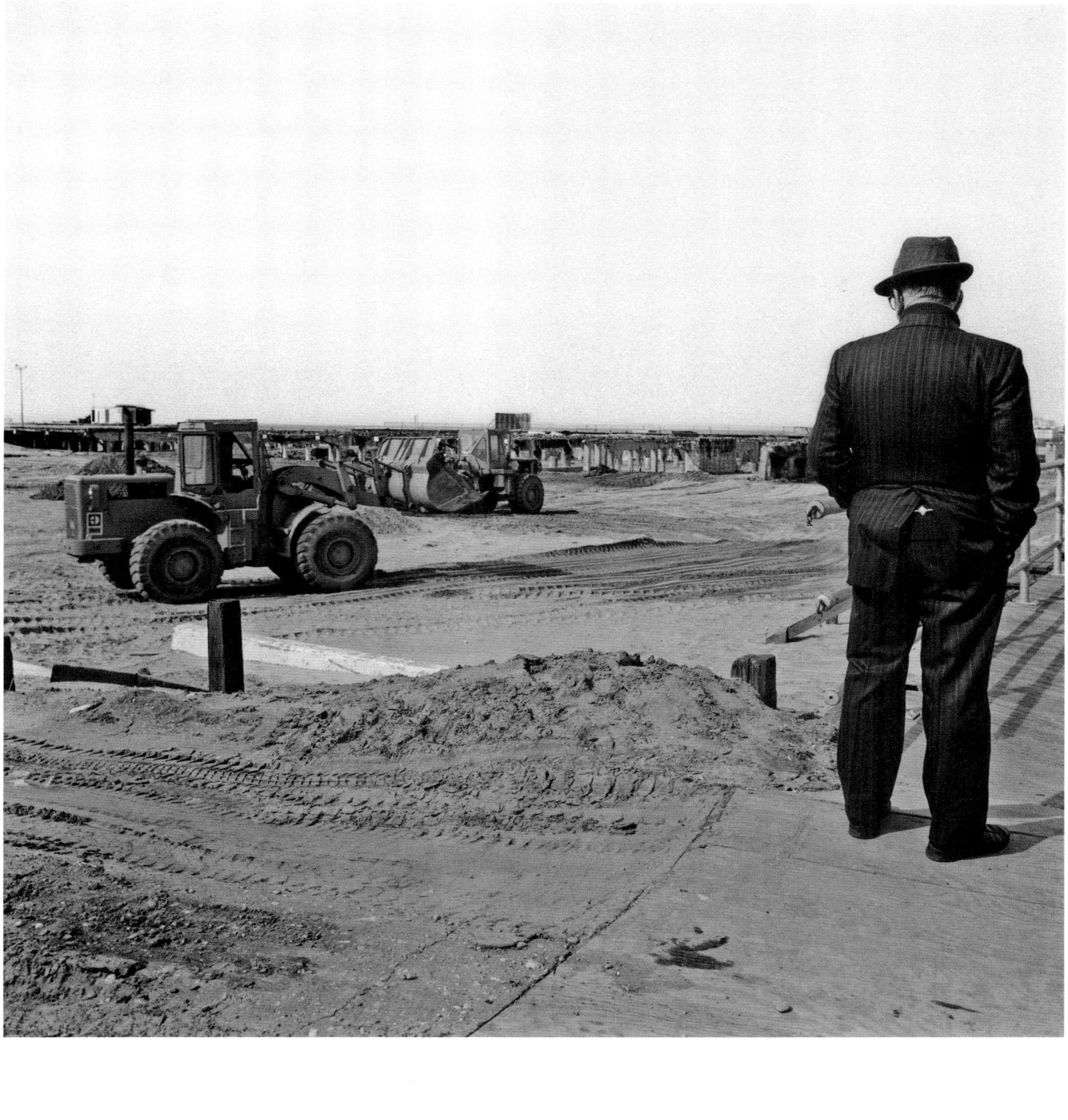

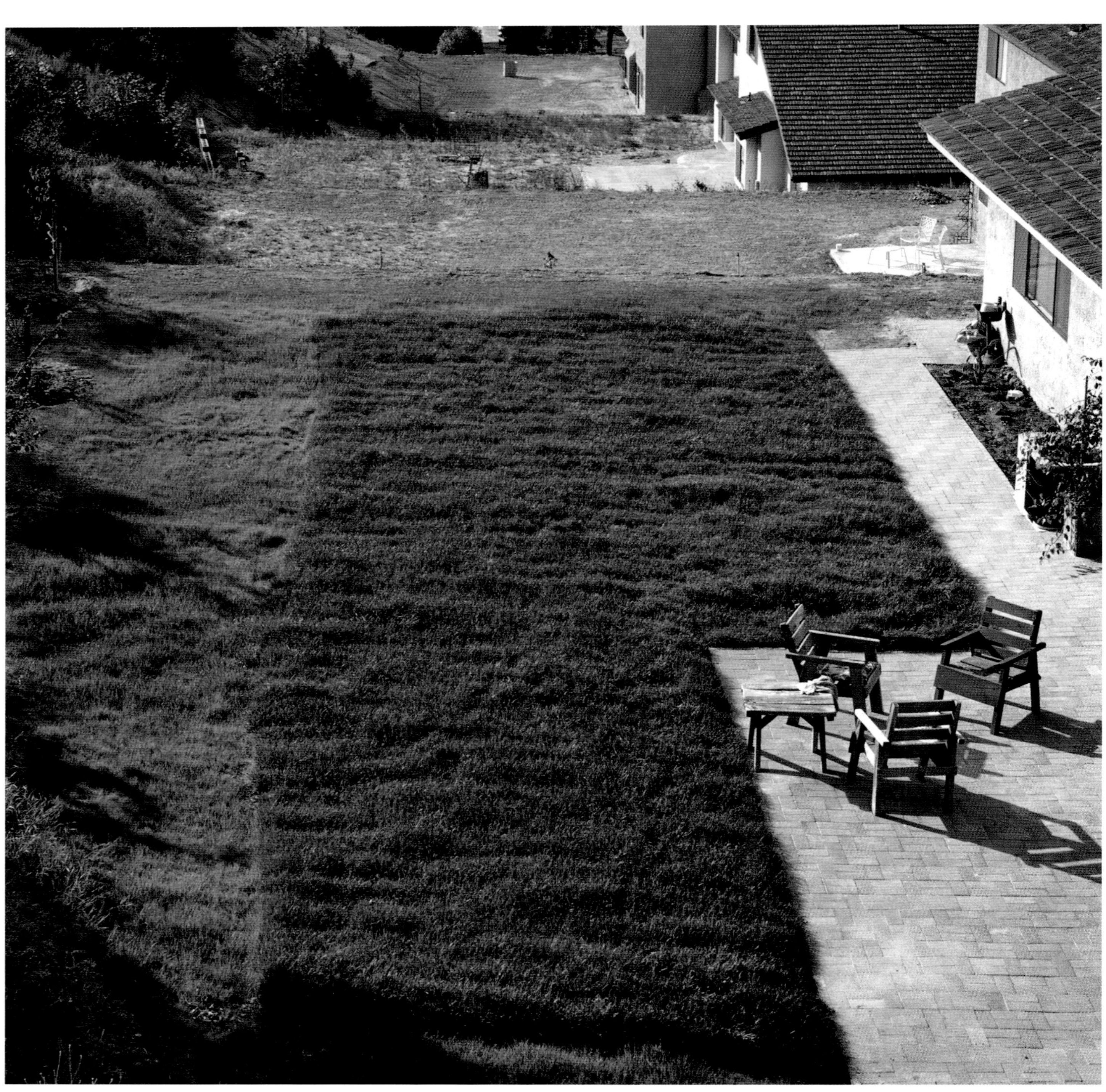

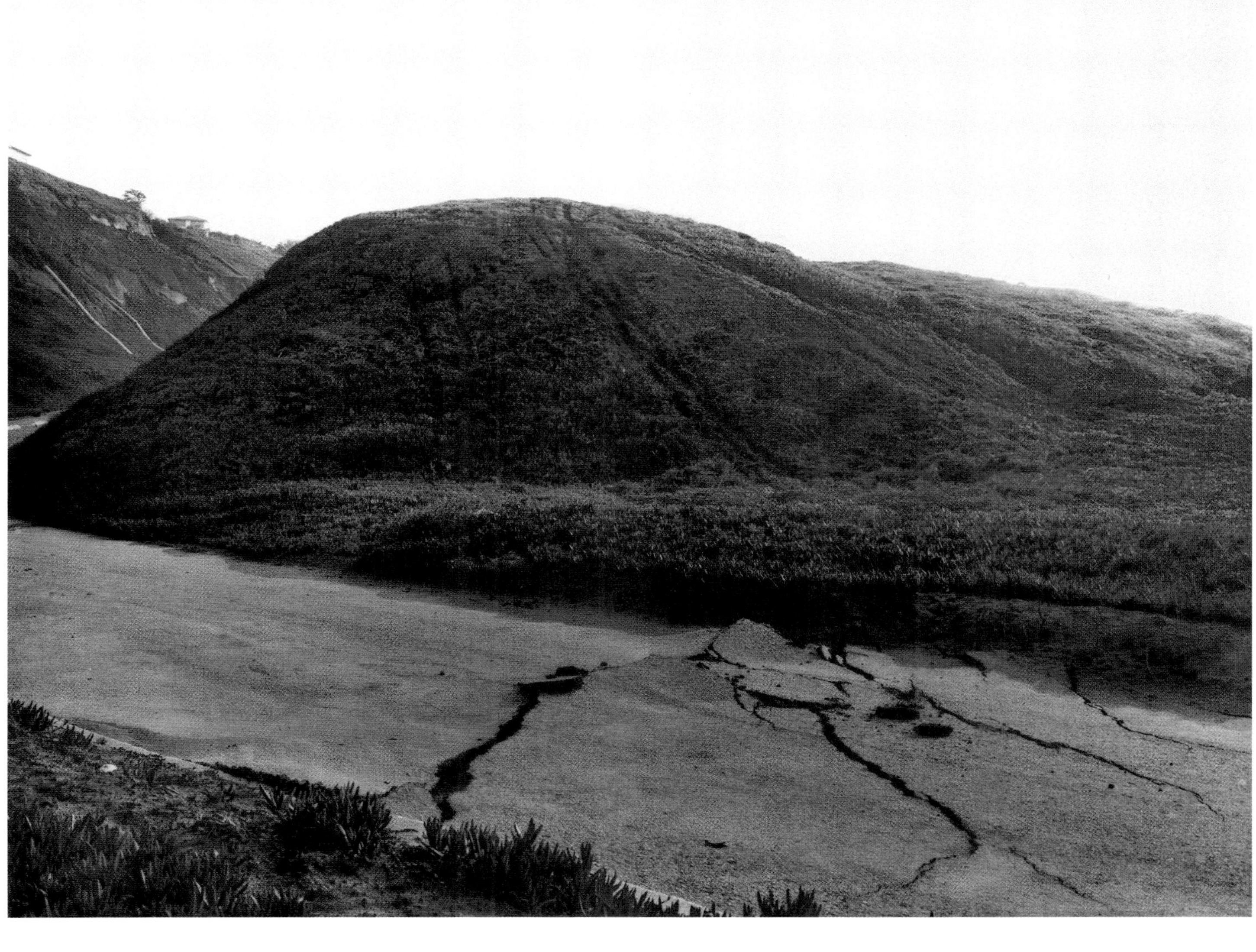

< Plate 43 **Joe Deal**, Backyard, Diamond Bar, California, 1980, Collection of David Knaus

^ Plate 44 **Peter Goin**, Mound and Walkway, Storm Damage at Thornton State Beach, 1983, UCR/ California Museum of Photography

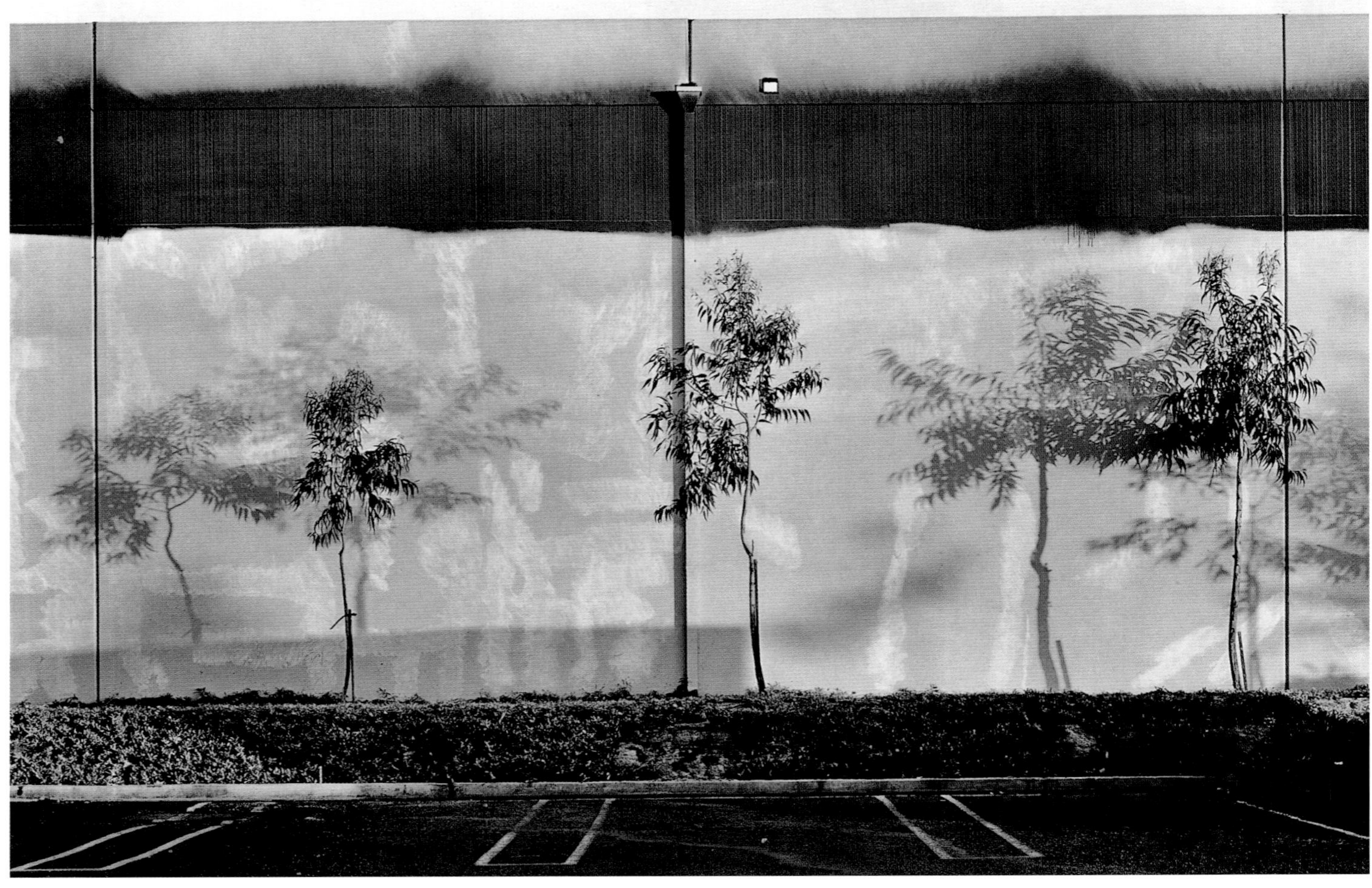

^ Plate 45 **Lewis Baltz**, 39. West Wall, Semicoa, 333 McCormick, Costa Mesa, *New Industrial Parks near Irvine, California* series, 1974, Orange County Museum of Art

> Plate 46 **Catherine Wagner**, Wall with Trees, 1976, Los Angeles County Museum of Art

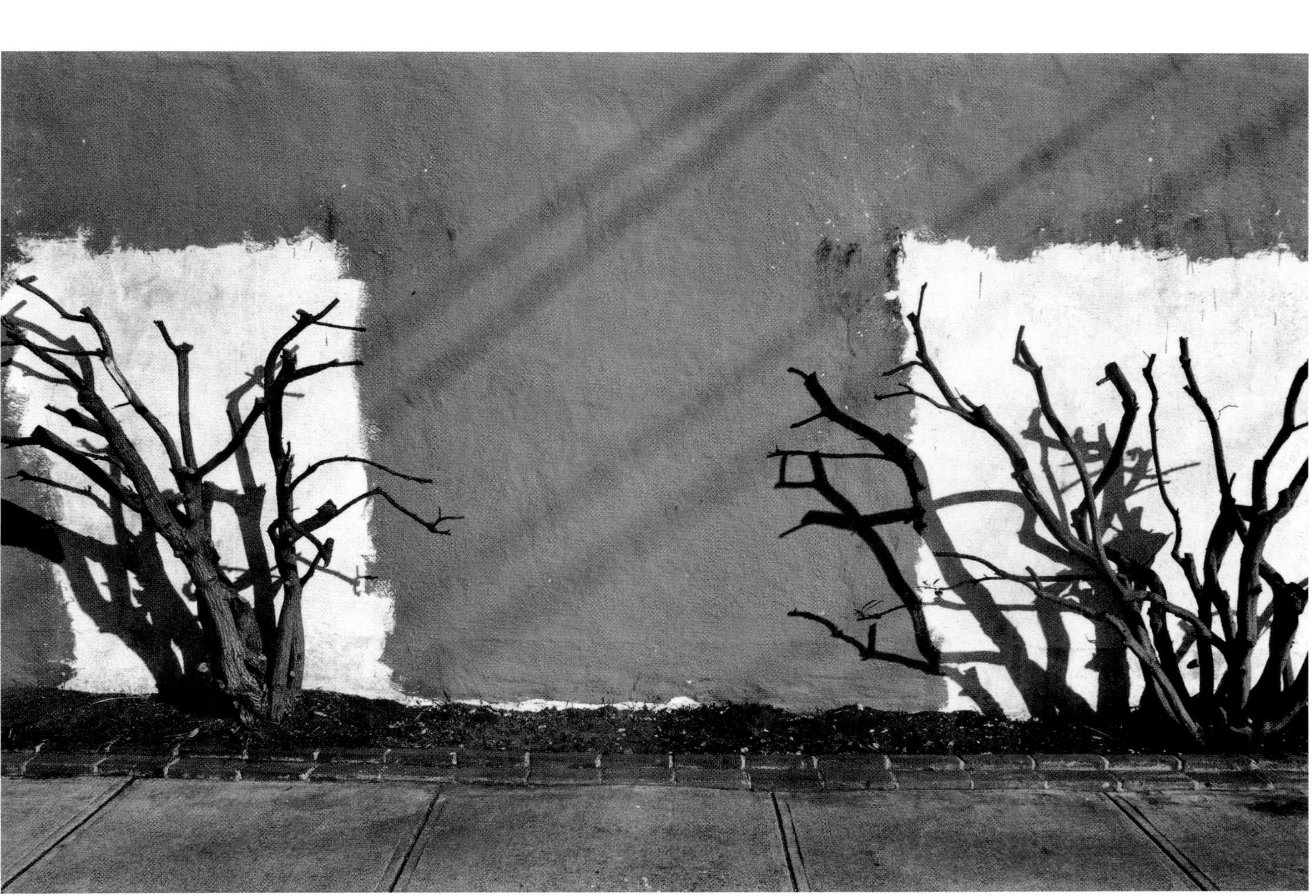

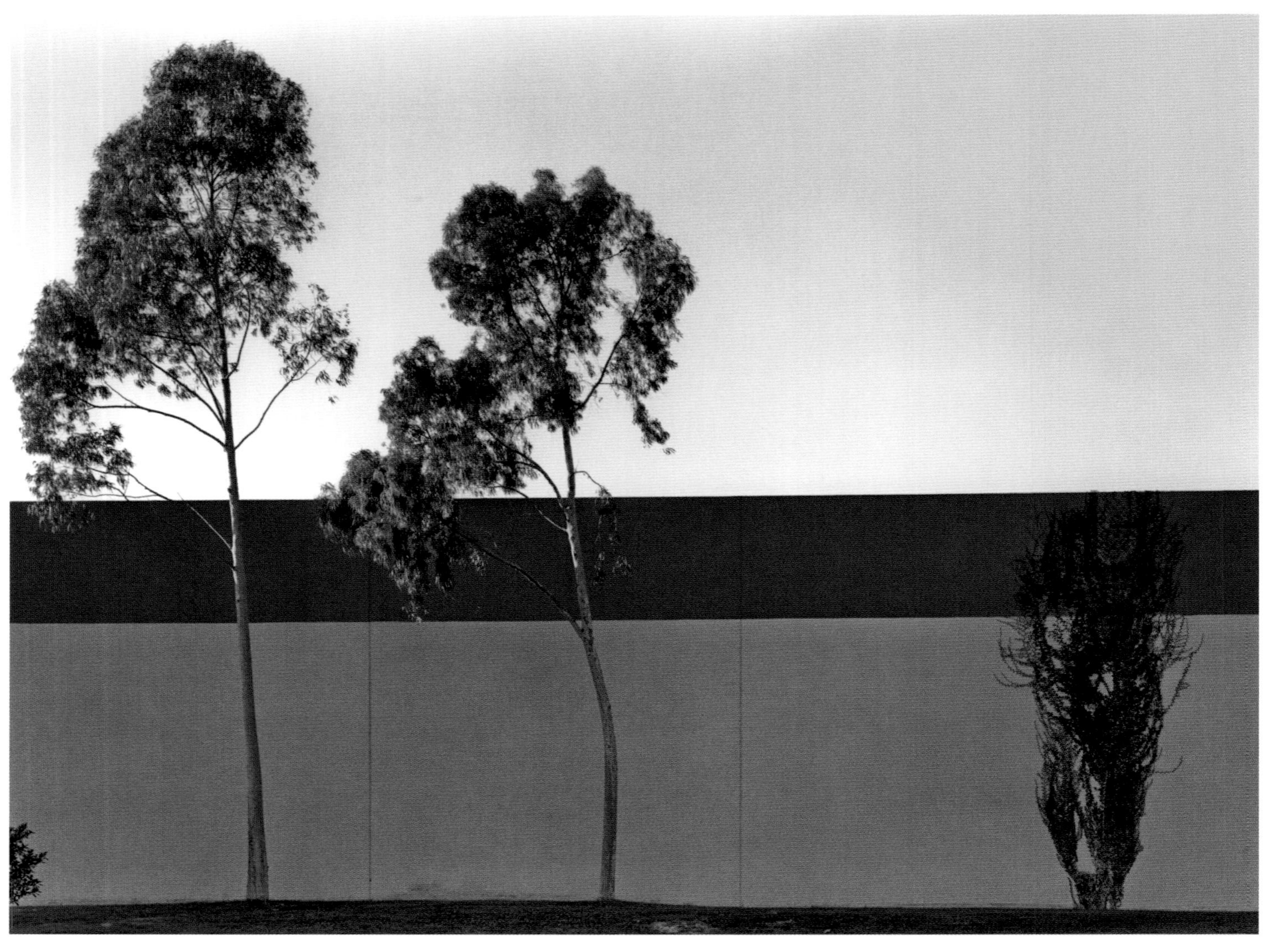

^ Plate 47 **Herb Quick**, Panco, Ltd., Irvine, California, 1981, *Sideviews* portfolio, UCR/California Museum of Photography

> Plate 48 **Mark Hinderaker**, untitled, 1970s, UCR/California Museum of Photography

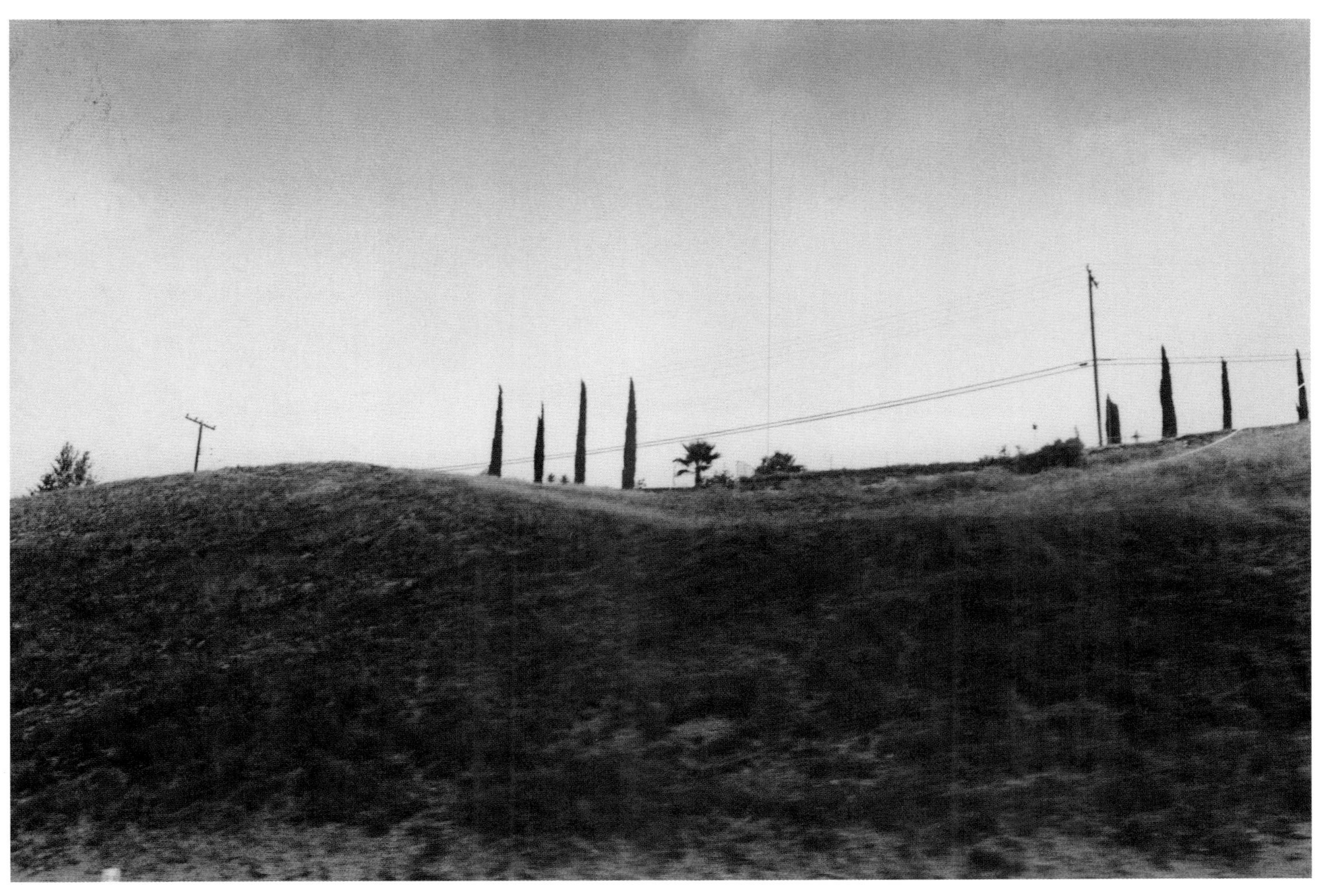

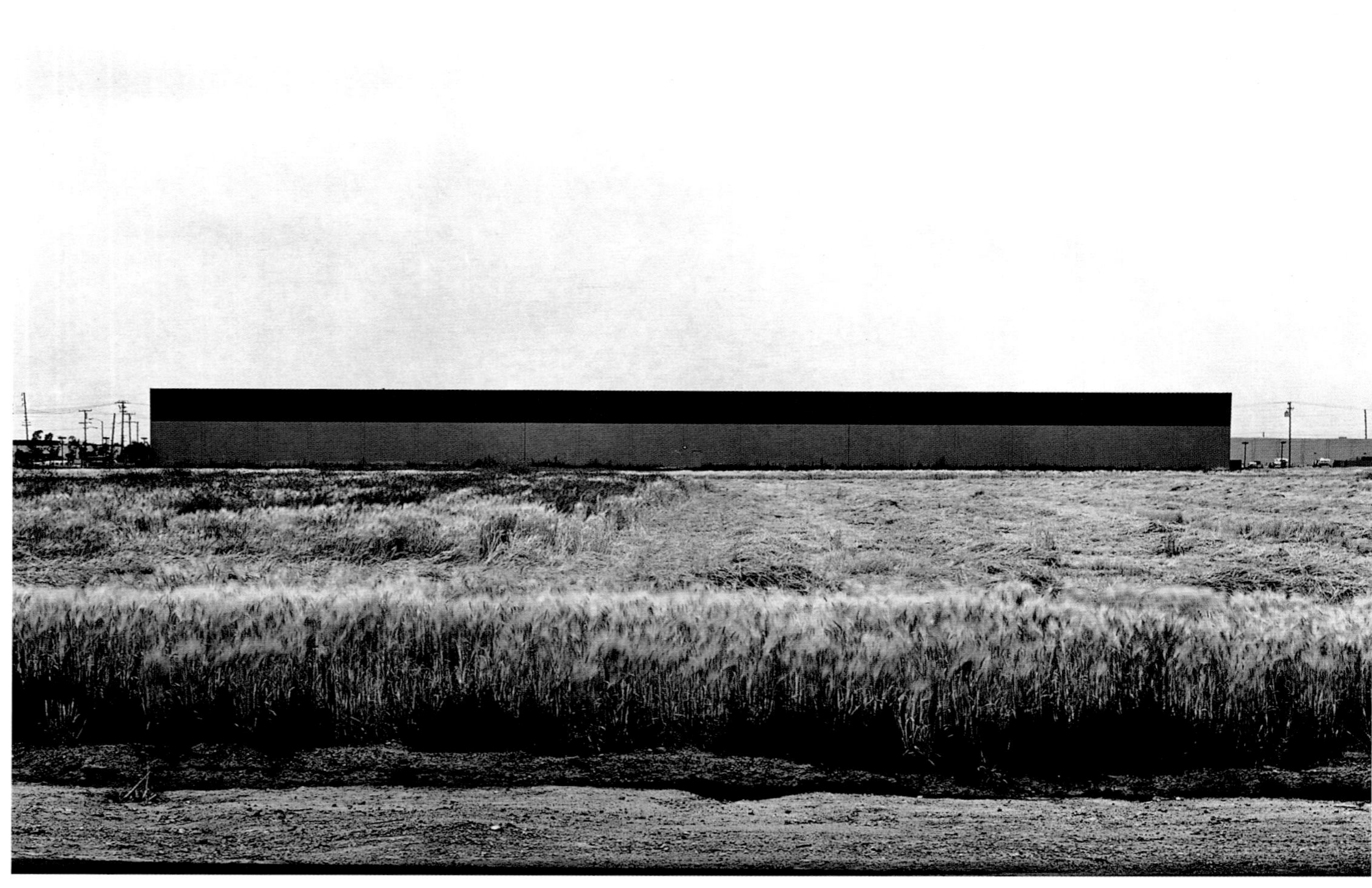

^ Plate 49 **Lewis Baltz**, 17. East Wall, Western Carpet Mills, 1231 Warner, Tustin, *New Industrial Parks near Irvine, California*, 1974, Orange County Museum of Art

> Plate 50 **Lewis Baltz**, 45. West Wall, Unoccupied Industrial Structure, 20 Airway Drive, Costa Mesa, *New Industrial Parks near Irvine, California*, 1974, Orange County Museum of Art

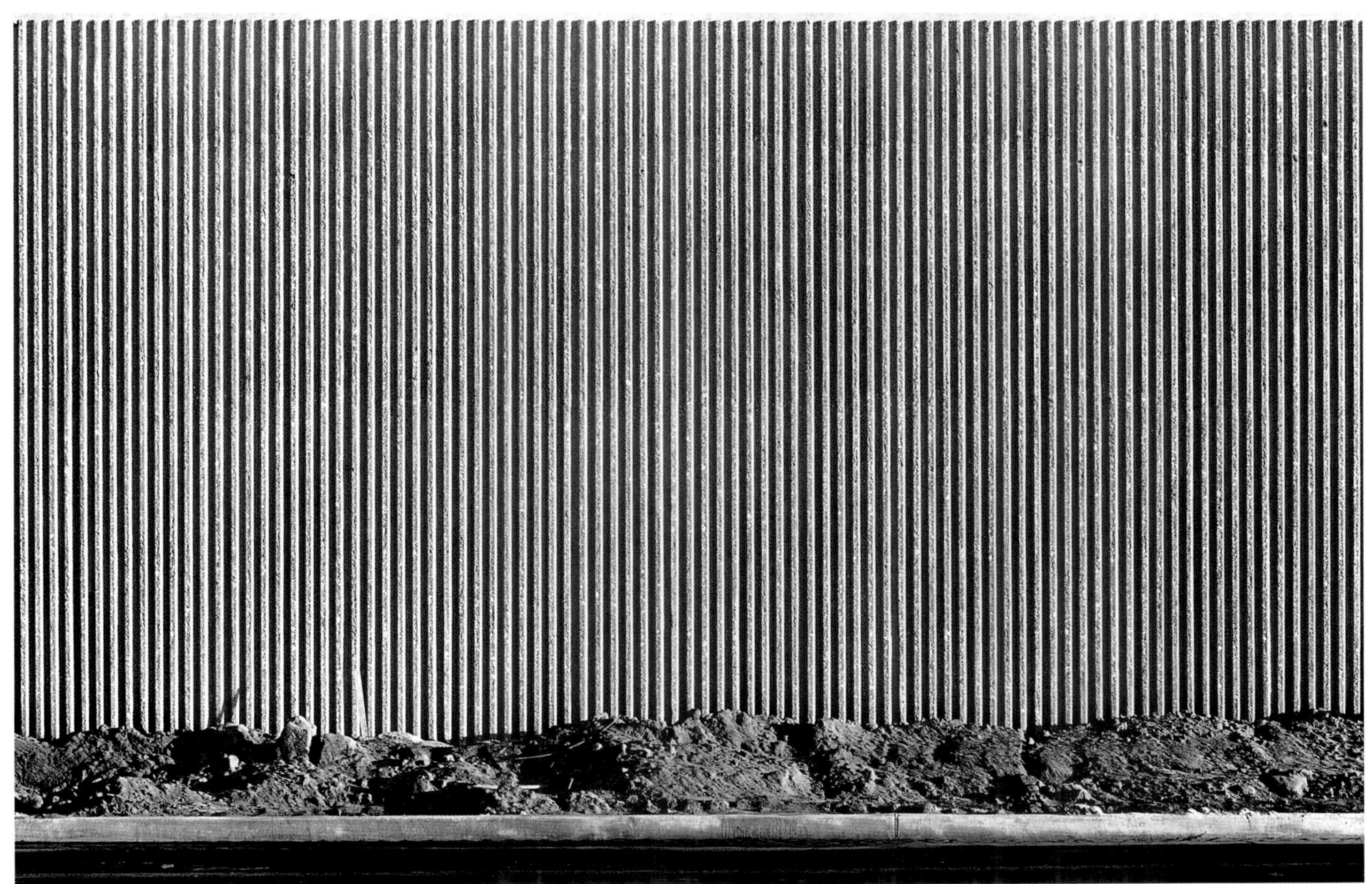

Joe Deal: My interest was what's on the ground, and I didn't like that the introduction of the sky turns the landscape into something else. I wanted to focus people's attention on what's on the ground. It allowed a kind of overall composition, where there's not one thing that's important and the rest isn't. When you have a horizon and you have deep space, the foreground elements take on a prominence that they don't have when you're up above, looking down.

The Fault Zone is horizonless. I'd take those maps that the LA County Engineer's Office gave me, and ... I'd look for something that was out of kilter some way or that was torn down, to just be suggestive. So you don't really see the evidence of an earthquake, because there weren't any to photograph. You see something that, in your mind, you have to transform into this threat overhanging the land.

It's among my favorite bodies of work, because it has that metaphorical quality that let me show how fragile the landscape is and how temporary. You have to be careful in a metaphorical series like this, that you're photographing subjects that are different enough, one from the other, that it doesn't become a series about trees or rocks.

WORKS IN THE EXHIBITION

All prints are gelatin silver unless otherwise noted.

Ansel Adams

Mount Williamson, Sierra Nevada, from Manzanar, California, 1944 (printed 1978), UCR/California Museum of Photography

Winter Sunrise, Sierra Nevada, from Lone Pine, California, 1944 (printed 1980), UCR/California Museum of Photography

Clouds Above Golden Canyon, Death Valley, California, 1946, Norton Simon Museum

Robert Adams

Ontario, California, 1983, J. Paul Getty Museum

Edge of San Timoteo, San Bernardino County, California, 1978, J. Paul Getty Museum

Orange Trees, Burned Palm, and Overturned Smudge Pot, Highlands, California, 1979, J. Paul Getty Museum

Palos Verdes, California, 1983, J. Paul Getty Museum

Area Recently Cleared of Citrus Groves, Redlands, California, 1980 (printed 1985), Fraenkel Gallery

Along Interstate 10, San Bernardino County, California, 1978 (printed 1979), Fraenkel Gallery

La Loma Hills, Colton, California, 1983 (printed 1980s), Fraenkel Gallery

Ontario, California, ca. 1980 (printed 1998) Fraenkel Gallery

anonymous

Atomic Crater, 1962, Collection of David Knaus

Lewis Baltz

Irvine Ranch, 1967, Los Angeles County Museum of Art

Irvine Ranch, 1968, Los Angeles County Museum of Art

Santa Cruz, 1970, Los Angeles County Museum of Art

Dana Point, no. 2, 1971, Los Angeles County Museum of Art

Mission Viejo, 1971, Los Angeles County Museum of Art

Fairfax, 1972, Los Angeles County Museum of Art

untitled, Marin County, 1983, *Sideviews* portfolio, UCR/California Museum of Photography

New Industrial Parks near Irvine, California series, 1974, Orange County Museum of Art (selections)

6. South Wall, PlastX, 350 Lear, Costa Mesa
7. Von Karmen Road between Alton and McGaw Roads, looking East
12. South Corner, Riccar America Company, 3184 Pullman, Costa Mesa
13. Deere Road between Damier and Red Hill Avenues, looking South
14. Foundation Construction, Many Warehouses, 2891 Kelvin, Irvine
15. West Wall, Space 18, 817 West 17th Street, Costa Mesa
17. East Wall, Western Carpet Mills, 1231 Warner, Tustin
20. Road Construction, Airport Loop Drive, Costa Mesa
21. Southwest Wall, Vollrath, 2424 McGaw, Irvine
24. East Wall, McGaw Laboratories, 1821 Langley, Costa Mesa
25. Kelvin between Derian and Jamboree Road, looking towards Newport Center
26. West Wall, R-ohm Corporation, 16931 Milliken, Irvine
27. Construction Detail, East Wall, Xerox, 1821 Dyer Road, Santa Ana
32. South Wall, Brinderson Mechanical Corporation, 100 East Baker, Costa Mesa
33. Barranca Road between Von Karman and Millikan Roads, looking Southwest
34. Millikin Road between Gates and DuBridge Roads, looking East
35. Jamboree Road between Beckman and Richter Avenues, looking Northwest
37. East Wall, Business Systems Division, Pertec, 1881 Langley, Santa Ana
39. West Wall, Semicoa, 333 McCormick, Costa Mesa
44. Unoccupied Warehouse, Santa Ana
45. West Wall, Unoccupied Industrial Structure, 20 Airway Drive, Costa Mesa
47. Window, Industrial Office, Newport Beach
51. South Wall, Resources Recovery Systems, 1882 McGaw, Irvine

Ruth Bernhard

Trees Reflected in Shaving Mirror, 1968, Norton Simon Museum

Michael Bishop

untitled (Floating Angels), 1969, Norton Simon Museum